Advance Praise for

The Power and Promise of Humane Education

This book should be required reading for every educator in the United States. Zoe Weil has laid out a practical guide for accessing complex issues in a manner that is thought-provoking, emotionally uplifting, and joyous. There is no school anywhere in the world that could not adopt at least some portion of the approaches articulated in this book and gift them to students who are, after all, the foundation for a humane future.

— DR. MICHAEL TOBIAS, President, Dancing Star Foundation

If only we had more writers like Zoe Weil explaining the message and philosophy of humane education. What a genuine revolution we would have in our schools and our hearts!

— COLMAN MCCARTHY, former *Washington Post* columnist, Director of the Center for Teaching Peace

Over 30 classroom years as a schoolteacher, and 18 more as a student, I became convinced that the familiar curriculum/ testing cycle of institutional schooling decisively unplugs children from humane goals, substituting memory for meaning and procedures for philosophy. In *The Power and Promise of Humane Education*, chock-full of nuts-and-bolts suggestions, Zoe Weil shows how we can redress the humane balance. Three cheers for this book – and for Zoe!

— JOHN TAYLOR GATTO, former New York State schoolteacher, author of *Dumbing Us Down: The Hidden Curriculum of Compulsory Schooling* and *The Underground history of American Education.*

The Power and Promise of Humane Education is another winner from Zoe Weil. It is practical, down-home and easy to read, a gold mine of information and, above all, inspirational. All educators and activists should read this book very carefully and share it widely. It is *that* good!

— MARC BEKOFF , author of *Minding Animals,* editor of the *Encyclopedia of Animal Behavior,* and cofounder with JANE GOODALL of Ethologists for the Ethical Treatment of Animals

The Power and Promise of Humane Education is the best introduction currently in existence to the understanding and practice of the exciting field of humane education. Educational pioneer Zoe Weil's skill at paving a more compassionate and interconnected way for education, through both her words and example, is at once extraordinary and greatly admirable.

— SANDRA HANNEN, President, New World Vision

A pleasure to read and filled with useful information and resources for everyone who cares about kids and the future of life on Earth, *The Power and Promise of Humane Education* is an incredibly important book. The longing to give and to serve is part of a child's essential nature, and this book provides insights and practical tools to awaken the highest values in children, helping to raise a new generation that thrives in service and contribution.

— OCEAN ROBBINS, Founder, Youth for Environmental Sanity, Author, *Choices For Our Future.*

The
power
and promise
of Humane Education

The
power
and promise
of Humane Education

Zoe Weil

NEW SOCIETY PUBLISHERS

Cataloguing in Publication Data:
A catalog record for this publication is available from the National Library of
Canada.

Cover design by Diane McIntosh. Cover image by Lanni Dimitroy/Alami.

Printed in Canada.

Paperback ISBN: 0-86571-512-2

Inquiries regarding requests to reprint all or part of *The Power and Promise* of
Humane Education should be addressed to New Society Publishers at the address
below.

To order directly from the publishers, please add $4.50 shipping to the price of
the first copy, and $1.00 for each additional copy (plus GST in Canada). Send
check or money order to:

New Society Publishers
P.O. Box 189, Gabriola Island, BC V0R 1X0, Canada
1-800-567-6772

New Society Publishers' mission is to publish books that contribute in fundamental
ways to building an ecologically sustainable and just society, and to do so with
the least possible impact on the environment, in a manner that models this vision.
We are committed to doing this not just through education, but through action.
We are acting on our commitment to the world's remaining ancient forests by
phasing out our paper supply from ancient forests worldwide. This book is one
step towards ending global deforestation and climate change. It is printed on acid-
free paper that is **100% old growth forest-free** (100% post-consumer recycled),
processed chlorine free, and printed with vegetable based, low VOC inks. For
further information, or to browse our full list of books and purchase securely,
visit our website at: www.newsociety.com

NEW SOCIETY PUBLISHERS   www.newsociety.com

Contents

Note

Those familiar with my previous book, *Above All, Be Kind: Raising a Humane Child in Challenging Times*, will find some of the same resources, activities, and background information here as well, primarily in the Resources section. While I wrote *Above All, Be Kind* to provide parents with the tools used by humane educators, *The Power and Promise of Humane Education* is primarily for teachers, educational reformers, and activists. Although the audiences for the two books are different, the themes are the same, which is why I've included some of the same resources for easy reference.

As midwives attending to the births of their students,
teachers carry an awesome responsibility, with corre-
spondingly awesome possibilities. Education, if it is to be
worthy of its true meaning, can, should, and must be at
the forefront of resistance to the routine dehumanization
of our industrialized mass culture ... There is much
work to be done. What are we waiting for?

— Derrick Jensen

Introduction

*"Only when we understand can we care; only when we
care shall we help; only if we help will all be saved."*

— Jane Goodall

As I WRITE THIS INTRODUCTION, I'm imagining you holding this book. You may be a teacher wondering what humane education is all about. You may be an activist hoping to educate others about the pressing issues that concern you. You may be an educational reformer or student of education wanting to create more effective and powerful curricula for meeting today's challenges. You may be a humane educator wanting new ideas. You may be a parent wishing to engage your children in an effort to create a better world. You may simply be a lifelong learner curious about humane education. Whether you are a teacher, activist, educational reformer, student, humane educator, parent, lifelong learner (or a combination of these), this book is for you. I have written it for two reasons. First, quite simply, I want to see the evolution of a peaceful and sustainable world, and that is what humane education promises to help create. Second, I would have liked to have a book to help me when I began my work in humane education in the mid 1980s, so I felt that it was time to share what I've learned in order to help others.

This book will give you ideas about and concrete examples of ways to teach about the most important issues of our time so that you will be part of a growing movement that is dedicated to bringing about a humane world through education. In the pages that follow you will find the tools to educate young people to be more humane so that together we can bring about such a world. I begin with a vision of what humane education is and what it has the potential to achieve. Next you'll find activities and lessons that you can use to put humane education into practice whether in classrooms, camps, nontraditional educational settings, after school programs, or homeschooling situations. Finally, you'll find information and resources that will help you become a more knowledgeable and effective humane educator.

I had wanted to write this book without listing the dangers we face on our planet and without sounding the alarm about the doomsday scenarios that could be our future. I did not want readers to open this book, sigh, and think, "Oh, not again. Please don't offer me a litany of horrors." Yet it is precisely the suffering, destruction, and cruelty on this planet that necessitate this book. It is because our world is still rife with violence and exploitation that we need humane education. I came to realize that I couldn't write this book without describing some of the problems in the world, because unless you agree that we confront serious challenges, you will not be convinced that humane education is so critical and necessary. With that said, I promise that I will confine the challenges we must address only to the next couple of pages. The rest of this book discusses humane education as the way to meet these challenges.

Here are just some of the problems we face:

- Thousands of species of plants and animals are becoming extinct every year, with thousands more threatened and in decline.
- Holes in the ozone layer of our atmosphere that protect life from harmful solar radiation continue to develop and grow.
- The vast majority of scientists agree that global warming is a serious and growing threat.

- Nuclear waste continues to be produced with no safe or permanent methods for storage or disposal.

- In 1900, the human population was approximately one and a half billion. In 1950, it grew to two and a half billion. The human population now exceeds 6 billion and will continue to grow into the foreseeable future. Even if we were all to live modestly, the Earth is unlikely to be able to support these numbers. As standards of living rise and more and more people emulate a consumer-based culture, the Earth's ecosystem will be unable to withstand such resource depletion, pollution, and production of solid, and often toxic, waste.

❖ ❖ ❖

- Warfare, terrorism, and violent answers to violent times are escalating around the globe as humans fail to achieve peaceful solutions to our conflicts.

- The disparity between rich and poor continues to grow around the world, paving the way for more conflict, suffering, inequity, and war.

- Human slavery is on the rise. Today, an estimated 27 million people, including children, are enslaved around the world. Slaves work in various industries, from brick and coal production to prostitution to farming.

- One quarter of the people on Earth do not have access to clean water.

- One billion people in the world are malnourished or starving.

- Sweatshops, where workers are not paid a living wage, are routinely fired for illness or pregnancy, and work 12- to-14-hour days, are proliferating around the globe. Many sweatshops employ children.

❖ ❖ ❖

- Tens of billions of chickens, turkeys, cows, pigs, and sheep are raised annually under cruel conditions before they are slaughtered for food. Factory farming accounts for the vast majority of modern agribusiness and includes severe confinement where animals are unable to move as well as mutilations such as branding, castration, tail removal, ear notching, and debeaking — all without pain relief or anesthesia.

- Tens of millions of nonhuman animals are used in product tests where they have chemicals, cosmetics, and household products dripped into their eyes, smeared on their shaved skin, or force-fed to them (all without anesthesia).
- More than five million dogs and cats are killed per year in the U.S. alone for lack of homes.
- More than one hundred million wild animals are killed in the U.S. by recreational hunters per year.
- Wild animals continue to be caught and stolen from their homes for zoos, circuses, sea parks, and the exotic pet trade.

This list could well go on and on. Many books have been written on each of these issues. However, this won't be one of them. Instead, this book offers a solution to all these problems: humane education. As a comprehensive field of study that draws connections between all forms of social justice, humane education examines what is happening on our planet, from human oppression to animal exploitation to ecological degradation. It explores how we might live with compassion and respect for everyone: not just for our friends, neighbors, and classmates, but for all people; not just for our own dogs and cats, but for all animals; not just for our school and home environments, but also for the Earth itself, our ultimate home. It invites students to envision creative solutions and to take individual action so that together we can bring about a world where kindness, integrity, and wisdom are the guiding principles in all our choices and relationships.

I wish that we did not need humane education, that it was enough to educate our children in the basics of language arts, science, math, social studies, and health, with plenty of room for the arts. But the times we are living in call upon us to teach young people about what is happening on this planet and to give them tools to make choices that will create a better, safer, more peaceful, and less cruel world. It is imperative that we commit ourselves to humane education. If we fail to teach the next generation how to be wiser decision-makers, we further imperil our world and all its inhabitants. In the face of war, bigotry, cruelty, and the destruction of our environment, humane education may be the most important subject we can teach.

Although I have called myself a humane educator for almost twenty years, for a long time I was uncomfortable with the word *humane*. The term *humane*, with *human* embedded in it, seemed to offer false hope for the problems we *humans* cause, and the struggles we *humans* face. Then one day I looked up the word *humane* in Webster's Collegiate dictionary and among the definitions I found this one: *"having what are considered the best qualities of human beings."* Humane education suddenly became so straightforward — my goal became to nurture the best qualities in students and to offer young people the tools to live accordingly.

And what are the best qualities that constitute being humane? After years of asking people to answer this question, I've generated the following list:

- Kindness
- Compassion
- Honesty and trustworthiness
- Generosity
- Courage
- Perseverance, self-discipline, and restraint
- Humor and playfulness
- Wisdom
- Integrity
- A willingness to choose and change

Ask students to write down their own answer to the question: "What are the best qualities of human beings," and, most likely, their lists will be similar to the one above, regardless of ethnicity, class, gender, or religion. I doubt very much that you will ever hear a student say "greed" or "cruelty." In our hearts and minds, each of us knows that kindness, compassion, and integrity are desirable attributes, and that wisdom and honesty are values worth cultivating.

Identifying humanity's best qualities provides a guide for young people's own lives, but knowing what it means to be humane is not enough. Without knowledge and critical thinking skills, without awareness of and access to humane choices, they won't really be able to put their list into practice in a very far-reaching way. For example, if a student writes "kindness" on her list, even if she is very kind in school and with her family, she is not fully living the value of kindness if she is buying a product that was produced through the labor of enslaved people half way around the world. But how would she know? Some of the kindest people I know — people who do not gossip, who have a warm smile for everyone, who are loving toward all whom they meet — live in ways that routinely cause significant suffering to others. We all do! Whether it's by using paper that comes from clearcut forests, purchasing products that pollute, buying clothes produced by exploited workers, eating factory farmed eggs and bacon at breakfast, even the kindest people can unwittingly cause harm. What humane education does is provide students with knowledge, awareness, and information-gathering skills so that they are able to choose to live according to their list of best qualities to the greatest extent possible.

Some may think that exposing young people to the ills of the world is harmful, not helpful. I share the concern that young children must be protected from too much knowledge about the suffering in the world, but elementary school students can certainly be inspired to live with compassion and kindness. As our children reach middle and high school, however, they will undoubtedly begin to know about the challenges we confront on this planet, whether or not we teach them about these ourselves. My experience has shown me that when humane educators impart information with the goal of inspiring positive solutions, rather than disempower youth, they empower them. Living according to our values, especially in the expansive way that humane education explores, is not easy, but it's exhilarating and deeply meaningful. The self-respect that a person who really strives to live according to her or his values develops is priceless. Despite what they know, despite the suffering and destruction they've been exposed to, young people who are offered humane education in age-appropriate ways usually become positive agents of change, and their cynicism and apathy diminish. They make wiser, kinder, more respectful decisions that better them as they better the world.

We have a clear, though challenging, task ahead of us. If we raise a generation to be truly wise and deeply compassionate, we can change the dangerous course we are on. To those who might think that we don't have enough time to educate the next generation with the knowledge and power to chart a different course (but instead must work to stop specific problems through legislation, activism, and other campaigns), I say that we don't have enough time *not* to teach our children to be humane. While it's essential that we continue to put out the fires of oppression and destruction, we need to stop the fires from spreading. Children who learn to live with genuine kindness toward others, to think critically about their choices and their lives, and to make wise decisions, help prevent future suffering and disaster.

Every teacher can be a humane educator. Whether in math, science, language arts, health, or social studies, humane education can become imbedded in the curricula so that it infuses the standard subjects. At the same time, humane education will achieve its greatest potential when courses taught by teachers specifically trained in humane education proliferate in the same number as math or social studies classes. Since the problems we face are so dire, so complex, and so interconnected, becoming a humane educator requires a thorough personal education on a host of issues: environmental ethics, human rights, culture and society, and animal protection. We need teachers who understand these subjects and the links between them, who have grappled with the complexities of these challenges as well as the conflicts that arise when trying to find solutions that are just and humane for all. It will be up to you to continually seek out information so that you can appropriately and powerfully educate your students and children. Humane educators do not simply send their students on the journey toward humane living — they go on the journey themselves. It is my hope that you will be inspired to keep learning more about these issues so that you can use the activities and ideas in this book to their fullest potential.

Some may think that we can't possibly add another subject, another set of standards, and another requirement for schools. If you are a teacher, you may feel weighed down by an additional burden being laid upon your shoulders when the task should be shared by parents and society in general. I agree that it must be shared, which is why I've also written a book for parents, *Above All, Be Kind: Raising a Humane Child in Challenging Times*, since raising a humane generation cannot be the job solely of teachers. But that doesn't mean that teachers don't have a crucial role to play in this profound task. And I am convinced that you will find humane education to be anything but a burden. It is an exciting, innovative, meaningful, and satisfying education that brings about such positive changes among young people that it becomes deeply rewarding and joyful work. Let it not be something that simply adds to your workload but something that ultimately enlivens and lightens it.

Part One

principles and practice

ONE

This Is Humane Education

"It is possible to mend wounds, to change minds, to minimize suffering. Our awareness makes it our responsibility to do so."

— Michael Tobias

The fifth graders at the Philadelphia school where I visited each month were rather rowdy when I walked into their classroom, but as I climbed onto their teacher's desk with a big plastic garbage bag in my hand, the room became hushed. After pausing dramatically atop the desk, I opened the bag, turned it upside down, and allowed the contents to spill out on the floor. A plastic milk jug, a trawl net float, 35 feet of nylon rope, a large blob of rubber, a spool of fishing line, two plastic soda bottles, several plastic grocery bags, a plastic cup and plate, and a piece of Styrofoam littered their classroom. Then I dropped the green trash bag itself, and it floated slowly to the floor.

After the shocked exclamations subsided I explained what these objects had in common. Items like them had been found inside a dying 28-foot sperm whale on a North Carolina beach. Veterinarians determined that the ingestion of all the garbage was the most likely cause of death.

These same students had learned about marine mammals in a previous class. They'd watched a film that described the vast migrations of the whales and heard the songs of the humpbacks. They'd grown to appreciate these intelligent mammals who live in the sea. Now they were learning about the threats to these animals — and they were fully engaged. I invited the students to come up and take an item from the floor back to their desks and asked them to take a few minutes to think about what else could have been done with it so that it wouldn't have wound up in the ocean killing a whale.

Students came up with great ideas. Some items could have been recycled or reused in obvious ways, but others required more creative thinking. One student said that the Styrofoam and fishing line could be used in art projects. Another commented that the plastic milk jug could have been made into a bird feeder. Most agreed that the items could have been kept out of the waste stream to begin with so that they would not have ended up in the ocean.

The students were fully involved in thinking about how to produce less garbage. They cared about the whale who died, and they recognized their part in protecting the environment and other animals.

This is humane education.

❖ ❖ ❖

Dani Dennenberg, a humane educator in San Diego, visits classrooms all over her county. In one class, she places the following objects on a table in front of the students:

- A box from a name brand athletic shoe
- The container for a fast food hamburger
- The wrapping of a commonly sold chocolate bar

Dani asks the students if they recognize these items, and all of them do. She asks if any of them have used, eaten, or purchased any of these items, and all their hands go up. Then she says to the class: "When you buy these products, you probably think that you are only buying the item inside, but you're actually buying more than that. I need three volunteers to come up and share with the class what else you're purchasing and to read aloud the other 'ingredients' in these products."

A girl comes up and opens the shoe box. On the inside of the box she sees some writing. Dani asks her to read it out aloud: "When you buy this item, in addition to getting the shoes themselves, you contribute to creating jobs for people and to economic growth. But you may also contribute to sweatshop labor, pollution, and animal suffering."

A boy opens the fast food container and reads: "When you buy this item, in addition to getting a tasty, convenient meal, you contribute to creating jobs for people and to economic growth. But you may also contribute to rainforest destruction, species extinction, the suffering of cows, pesticide use, water waste, pollution, increases in heart disease, cancer, obesity, and strip mall development."

A third student comes up, opens the chocolate bar wrapper and reads: "When you buy this item, in addition to getting a delicious dessert, you contribute to creating jobs for people, to economic development, and to world trade. But you may also contribute to child and slave labor."

Dani spends the next twenty-five minutes discussing the issues raised by the packaging "ingredients." She explains how children in West Africa, many of them slaves, gather cocoa beans that wind up in our chocolate, how many name brand athletic shoes are made in sweatshops, and how the production of fast foods raises environmental, health, human rights, and animal welfare questions. Then Dani describes alternatives that contribute to economic health and personal happiness and well-being without causing so much harm to other people, animals, or the environment.

This is humane education.

❖ ❖ ❖

Melissa Feldman, a teacher in Boston, begins a class by holding up a shopping bag from Tiffany's and asking a group of tenth grade students, "If you saw me at the mall carrying this bag, what would you think of me?" Next she holds up a bag from Victoria's Secret, and asks the same question. Finally she holds up a bag from Wal-Mart and asks again. The students are quite adept at generating stereotypes about the kind of person who would carry each bag. When she asks the students, "How did you know about each bag?" their answer is "Advertising." To illustrate the pervasiveness of advertising in their lives, Melissa "tests" her students' advertising knowledge. She holds up a poster that lists familiar advertising slogans. Each slogan has a word missing, and she asks the students to supply the missing word. For example, "Got ___?" (answer: milk). Next she holds up a poster with several enlarged letters from products, such as the "M" from McDonald's, the "G" from the Gap, and the "C" from Crest. Students shout out the product names just from seeing a single letter. She does the same with logos, such as the Nike swoosh or the Target bull's eye. Students easily demonstrate how well-trained they are by advertisers.

After these "tests," Melissa asks, "How did all this advertising get into your brains?" and helps the students generate a list of marketing strategies that are used to turn us all into faithful consumers of brand name products. Melissa explains that she is quite familiar with all of these methods because for many years she used them in her work. She tells the students about her job as a former model and fashion coordinator for a clothing designer, and explains that when she was in her twenties she produced advertising that promoted a very specific and narrow image of women. She encouraged women to buy the latest, newest, coolest fashions that her company manufactured in China. She advertised fur and ivory. She told sixteen-year-old girls that their bodies weren't good enough to be in her ads or fashion shows. She lets the class know that back then she never even bothered to learn these girls' names.

Then Melissa tells the class that she came to realize her life was filled with very superficial concerns. Obsessed with her weight and her looks, eager to befriend those who were beautiful and successful, and uninterested in others who did not fit her image of prestige and glamour, she began to feel that her life was meaningless and shallow. She had started to become aware of the suffering of people and animals in our world and concerned about environmental problems, so one day she decided to leave her lucrative profession and do something that mattered.

Melissa lets the students know that she's now trying to undo the message she once promoted by teaching young people how to scrutinize information with a critical eye and to uncover the hidden links between our product choices and the suffering they may cause to others.

This is humane education.

❖ ❖ ❖

Matt Wildman, a teacher at a Brooklyn high school, taught a year-long course on justice and empathy that became one of the most popular classes at the school. The class met every day and covered such topics as prejudice, consumerism, human rights, the environment, animal protection, and world conflicts.

In one class, Matt explored the concept of apathy. He read aloud the famous story of Kitty Genovese, a Queens woman attacked and killed late at night outside her apartment building. The attack against her lasted over thirty minutes, and despite her screams she was ignored by dozens of her neighbors. Following the classroom reading on Ms. Genovese's death, the students wrote their personal reflections on this horrifying murder. Then they explored the psychological conditions that lead to apathy. Matt invited the students to think about situations in their own lives when they experienced feelings of apathy and to reflect upon why they had these feelings, and what would have engaged and motivated them. Throughout the rest of the year, as they studied various issues and problems in the world, the students made connections between Ms. Genovese's story and the plight of other people as well as that of animals endeavoring to survive.

This is humane education.

❖ ❖ ❖

"Which choice helps more, and harms less?" Freeman Wicklund, an educator from Minneapolis, asks a group of junior high students as he hands out a stack of cards. Printed on each card is a choice between two similar products or activities. Some of the cards read:

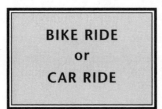

> BIKE RIDE
> or
> CAR RIDE

> CLEANING SOLUTION OF BAK-
> ING SODA AND WATER
> or
> CONVENTIONAL SCOURING
> POWDER

> FAIR TRADE, SHADE
> GROWN, ORGANIC
> COFFEE
> or
> CONVENTIONAL COFFEE

Freeman invites the students to think about the products and activities on the cards in relation to other people, other species, and the Earth. He teaches the students what concepts like "fair trade" and "shade grown" mean. He has learned about these terms and issues himself and is able to answer students' questions accurately and to provide the background information necessary for them to determine which choices harm less and help more.

Some of the Choices Cards introduce words or concepts that are less obvious, such as:

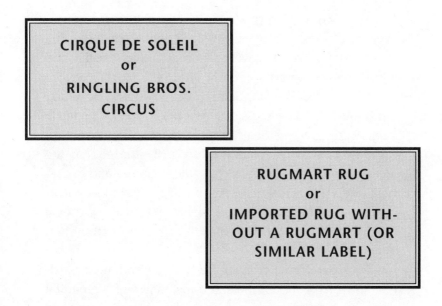

```
CIRQUE DE SOLEIL
       or
RINGLING BROS.
    CIRCUS
```

```
RUGMART RUG
       or
IMPORTED RUG WITH-
OUT A RUGMART (OR
 SIMILAR LABEL)
```

Freeman explains that Cirque de Soleil is a circus troupe that relies upon human talent rather than animal acts to entertain audiences and that Rugmart is a label that ensures that a rug is made by people who work under decent conditions and receive fair wages. After he's answered students' questions, they use the information to decide which choice harms less.

In just a few minutes, the students in Freeman's class have considered the impact of various products and actions on the environment, animals, and people around the world. They have learned that their own choices can make a difference. Freeman hasn't told the students which choices to make, but he has asked them to think about choices in a new way, based upon their impact on others.

This is humane education.

THE POWER AND PROMISE OF HUMANE EDUCATION
PROFILE 1: SCOTT

When he was in 11th grade, Scott took a humane education elective taught at his high school in Maine. The semester-long course covered human rights, media and culture, environmental ethics, and animal protection. When the course began, Scott was fairly quiet. He didn't contribute to class discussions very often. As the semester progressed, however, Scott became more and more enthusiastic and participated fully in class. By the end of the course, he was coming into class full of energy and excitement and was a vocal defender of the power of individuals to make a difference in the world. He made personal changes in his life that reflected his growing compassion and respect for others.

As he describes it, the course "helped lead me towards a life in which consciousness and awareness of the natural world are essential and valued." The class also inspired Scott to choose as his senior project the topic: "What Is Wrong with Our Treatment of the World." Scott examined various issues — including global warming, agricultural runoff in the Gulf of Mexico, habitat destruction and over-development, the ozone holes, and endangered species — and attempted to present an overview of the consequences of human actions.

Scott has just started college and plans to pursue environmental studies. He says, "I intend to incorporate environmentally and morally sound practices into whatever field I end up working in."

TWO

The Four Elements of Humane Education

"Why is compassion not part of our established curriculum, an inherent part of our education? Compassion, awe, wonder, curiosity, exaltation, humility — these are the very foundation of any real civilization, no longer the prerogatives of any one church, but belonging to everyone, every child in every home, in every school."
— Yehudi Menuhin

Over the years, I've come to identify four elements that form the foundation of quality humane education:

1. **Providing accurate information** so students understand the consequences of their decisions as consumers and citizens.
2. **Fostering the 3 Cs: Curiosity, Creativity, and Critical Thinking** so students can evaluate information and solve problems.

3. **Instilling the 3 Rs: Reverence, Respect, and Responsibility** so students will act with kindness and integrity.
4. **Offering positive choices that benefit oneself, other people, the Earth, and animals** so students feel empowered to help create a more humane world.

While each element is important in itself, it is the combination of these four elements that makes humane education so effective and powerful. Without information we are unable to make thoughtful decisions. Without curiosity, creativity, and critical thinking, our decisions may be unwise. Without reverence we may not care enough to extend our compassion; without respect we may be unable to reign in our desires and impulses; without responsibility, we may fail to rise to the enormous task before us as humans living on a beleaguered planet. And without positive choices, we may succumb to despair. When we are offered these four elements, however, we are empowered to learn, think, care, and act, with the best qualities of human beings as our guide.

SWBATBK

SWBAT is an acronym that teachers sometimes use to help identify their objectives in a lesson plan. It stands for: "Students Will Be Able To." For example, a biology teacher might have as an objective that students will be able to accurately explain the process of photosynthesis. A language arts teacher might have as a goal that students will be able to identify the parts of a sentence. My acronym for humane educators is quite a mouthful: SWBATBK — students will be able to be kind. Through the Four Elements humane education gives students the knowledge, the critical thinking skills, the inspiration, and the choices in order to actually *be* kind and put their values into practice. It provides the crucial signposts on their map so that they can reach the destination of living humanely.

Element 1: Providing Accurate Information

Because humane education's goal is to promote humane choices and humane citizenship, it must cover a broad spectrum of issues. To help students become aware and thoughtful consumers of things such as food, clothing, housing, transportation, entertainment, and products of all kinds, humane educators need to provide young people with accurate information relevant to these choices. While humane educators may specialize in different areas, they share the goal of providing information about suffering and harm so that students can make more compassionate and respectful decisions.

So, for example, humane educators might teach about:

- Advertising, media, and public relations, to determine the ways in which our choices are influenced by companies wishing to sell products and affect behaviors
- Multinational monopolies and corporate influences in government and schools, to explore the ways in which our cultural ideals, education, and the political process are molded by profit-making
- Sweatshops, slavery, and child labor around the world
- Racism, sexism, homophobia, jingoism, and other prejudices that diminish people's lives and cause oppression and exploitation
- Global warming, pollution, resource depletion, deforestation, and species extinction
- Genetic engineering of foods, aquaculture, factory farming, soil erosion, the growing scarcity of fresh water, and the decline of productive agricultural land
- Animal exploitation and cruelty in various industries and forms of entertainment.

Unfortunately, information relevant to humane decision-making is often hidden or hard to find in the mainstream media or, for that matter, in schools. Whether the information concerns the effects of our choices on the environment, on communities of people around the world, on our own health, or on nonhuman animals, without a significant effort at information-gathering, most of us will likely remain in the dark. Humane educators gather information — making sure that it is accurate and from reputable sources — and teach students how to become information-gatherers themselves so that they learn what they need to know in order to make humane choices in relation to themselves and others.

Here are a few examples of information that has largely been left out of the mainstream media:

1. Until 2000, few knew much, if anything, about the increase in slavery in many countries. Kevin Bales' *Disposable People* as well as a few publicized investigations into slave labor on West African cocoa plantations and in the Sudan, brought public attention to an atrocity that has been growing for decades. According to Bales, there are more slaves today than there were during the peak of the African slave trade in the 17th and 18th centuries. Yet most people probably believe that slavery was eradicated over a century ago.

2. Before the humanitarian Henry Spira took out a full-page ad in the *New York Times* in 1980 that included a photo of a rabbit and the question, "How many rabbits does Revlon blind for beauty's sake?" few realized that companies producing cosmetics and personal care and cleaning products were testing them on animals. These companies had been pouring shampoos, perfumes, oven cleaners, and scouring powders into the eyes of unanesthetized rabbits and force-feeding animals lethal quantities of these substances for decades. Most of the large companies producing such products *still* conduct these tests, killing millions of animals in testing laboratories every year.

3. In 1992, a document titled "World Scientists' Warning to Humanity" was released. It was signed by more than sixteen hundred scientists, including over half of all living Nobel Prize winners, from seventy-one different countries. The document began with these words:

> Human beings and the natural world are on a collision course. Human activities inflict harsh and often irreversible damage on the environment and on critical

resources. If not checked, many of our current practices put at serious risk the future that we wish for human society and the plant and animal kingdoms, and may so alter the living world that it will be unable to sustain life in the manner that we know. Fundamental changes are urgent if we are to avoid the collision our present course will bring about. (Quoted in David Suzuki, *The Sacred Balance*, Prometheus Books, 1998, p. 4.)

Hardly any media carried this story or printed this document, despite the fact that such a statement by so many scientists was unprecedented and that the warning quite extreme.

Students usually look forward to humane education classes. The biggest reason why is perhaps because humane educators expose them to hidden information that, however disturbing, is important. By uncovering information that is otherwise difficult to obtain, humane educators enable students to address relevant and pressing issues, and students generally find this very meaningful. But if humane education simply exposes students to the suffering and destruction in our world, it can be unproductive at best and psychologically damaging at worst. Providing accurate information is only the first step in humane education. The purpose of providing that information is to spark creative and critical thinking and to pave the way for new and more humane choices.

Element 2: Fostering the 3 Cs: Curiosity, Creativity, and Critical Thinking

Advertisements from popular teen magazines are spread all over the floor of a classroom as groups of four to five eleventh graders analyze the messages embedded in them. The humane educator has written the following questions on the board:

1. What product or service is the ad selling?
2. What deep need or desire is the ad appealing to?
3. Who is the intended audience, and what do you suppose their

reaction to the ad might be?
4. Who is excluded by the ad?
5. How does the ad affect your personal desires, self-image, beliefs, and consumer choices?
6. What are the effects of the product or service the ad is selling on people, other species, and the environment, and what suffering, destruction, and/or exploitation remains unseen?

You might find some of these questions in a media literacy class, but what makes this a humane education activity is the emphasis on who is affected by advertising and hidden suffering and destruction. Learning to analyze advertising carefully helps students recognize beliefs masquerading as facts. By thinking critically, students become empowered to seek truth in an enduring way that enables them to be less encumbered by the messages in advertising and more able to rely upon their own deepest values. In practical terms, they may no longer be taken in by ads or buy the latest fad items.

One ad the students in this class examine depicts a young white man meditating in the lotus position in front of a Ford truck and a huge pile of stuff, mostly sports equipment of every variety. The copy reads: "Spence put a new twist on an old philosophy. To be one *with* everything, he says, you've gotta have one *of* everything. That's why he also has the new Ford Ranger. So he can seek wisdom on a mountain top. Take off in hot pursuit of enlightenment. And connect with Mother Earth. By looking no further than the planet's coolest 4-door compact pickup. He says it gives him easy access to inner peace. Which makes him one happy soul."

While media literacy techniques would help students analyze the messages in the ad and recognize the ways in which the ad manipulates young white males into wanting a Ford Truck, humane education also invites students to think about the ad's effects on other species, other people, and the Earth. The message that we in industrialized countries should aspire to have one of everything in order to be fully developed human beings (however humorous the ad) is not only damaging to our own souls, it threatens the survival of countless species and the health of the environment. A world in which every person seeks to have one of everything is a world that depletes its resources, pollutes its air, water, and land, and causes the extinction of plants and animals. Then there is the gas-guzzling truck itself, pictured in the wilderness, with no reference to the damage that automobiles, especially SUVs and trucks, cause to the environment and to human health. Granted, the ad is tongue-in-cheek, yet the message that materialism brings happiness is ubiquitous in our society.

All these potential negative effects are hidden until students pause to really look at and assess the messages that bombard them. Once they do so, they can creatively address the issues raised by advertising. On the one hand, free speech is one of our most important freedoms, and few want to risk the heavy hand of Big Brother by constraining advertising. On the other hand, advertising's manipulations indirectly cause a host of concerns. "Perhaps," suggests one student, trying to come up with a creative solution, "advertisers could be required to print warning labels on products, like they do with cigarettes, or would have to include the true cost of the product on the environment, animals, and people working in the factories that produce the product."

Humane educators encourage their students to think critically not only about advertising, products, and attitudes, but also about the information they themselves are presenting. Good humane educators don't want their students to blindly believe them any more than they want their students to blindly believe the public relations materials from Monsanto. I often begin humane education classes by telling the students that I don't want them to believe a word I say. Instead, I want them to be able to approach any information, whether from a trusted teacher, a respected scientist, or the *National Enquirer*, with the tools to assess that information for themselves. I want them to be curious about the sources of information, critical about what's presented to them, and creative in their efforts to solve problems.

Element 3: Instilling the 3 Rs: Reverence, Respect, and Responsibility

While schools endeavor to teach the 3 Rs of reading, writing, and arithmetic, humane educators try to instill an additional 3 Rs: reverence, respect, and responsibility. Without these three Rs, the problems of our world, from human oppression to environmental destruction to animal cruelty, will inevitably continue. Although we need good information and creative and critical thinking skills to address problems, these are not sufficient. Each of us also must feel inspired to take responsibility for the challenges that confront us. That inspiration usually comes from our own reverence and respect for the Earth and all of its inhabitants.

REVERENCE

Reverence is an emotion akin to awe. What we revere, we honor deeply and are likely to protect and cherish. If children's reverence for the natural world, for animals, for the good in human beings, and for peace is cultivated and nurtured, they will likely make choices that reflect their reverence, which will, in turn, create a more compassionate and peaceful world. When we feel reverence, our lives are enriched, our experiences are touched with power and purpose, and our actions are permeated with respect.

To nurture reverence, you can bring activities and meaning into the classroom that inspire compassion and appreciation and explore the ways in which all life is inextricably connected, mysterious, and awe-inspiring. (Parents can do this at home as well.)

In middle and high school social studies or language arts classes, you might inspire reverence in the classroom

- By showing a video about Mahatma Gandhi or the young Canadian human rights activist Craig Kielburger
- By creating a modern-day scenario of the underground railroad
- By recounting the heroic efforts of activists to stop the clubbing of seals on the ice floes in the North Atlantic

- By telling stories about especially kind or noble people.

In science classes, you can inspire reverence in the classroom

- By showing films about the rainforests and sharing the successes of children who are protecting large tracts of tropical forests
- By relating accounts of remarkable examples of animal communication
- By countless experiments in which students explore the mystery and wonder of life without harming life in the process
- By growing herbs and vegetables in a school garden
- By quoting scientists whose discoveries led them to more humanitarian beliefs (for example, scientists who dispelled the myth of "race" by explaining that physical differences in human beings lie along a continuum and are not meaningful distinguishing characteristics).

None of these activities are particularly unusual, and in fact, you may already use them. Some may read this list and feel excited to try new activities, while others might think, "I've done this stuff, and my students are still apathetic and not at all reverent." Often, when teachers bring reverence-inspiring activities to students, it helps to set a tone in the classroom that what is about to happen is different. By letting students know that you will not be testing them, and that they don't have to take notes, and by inviting them to experience something new in an otherwise routine day, you will help set the stage for feelings of reverence. You can begin by turning off the fluorescent lights and lighting a candle, moving the chairs into a circle, and sharing an extraordinary story. Or you can tell your students that they are about to see film footage that was taken undercover and that they were never supposed to see. Even the smallest changes to the norm in the classroom may set the stage for reverence-inspiring activities.

While reverence can be fostered in the classroom, confining these activities to within the school walls does not lend itself to the breadth and depth of the reverence that could be cultivated through field trips. If social studies teachers want to motivate their students to be good citizens, then a trip to visit those whose lives are dedicated to improving the world may be just the inspiration they need. Meeting activists who attempt to solve the problems of our time with creativity and commitment helps young people realize that they, too, can use their creative energies to come up with ideas to help. Visiting a homeless shelter where students get to hear from those who have lost their homes and from the volunteers who are trying to help elicits children's compassion and may inspire them to make a difference themselves. A visit with a Holocaust survivor will leave an indelible impression on students who may be motivated to fight for social justice. Hearing the story of a former criminal who turned his life around to help others will remind students that all of us can change.

If teachers want their students to feel wonder about the miracle of life and the beautiful complexity of nature, then the place to awaken that wonder is in nature. There are numerous outdoor games and activities that inspire reverence in the guise of play. I've included one of them below, and three more can be found in the Activities section (pp. 107-109). There are also many books with nature activities for children (see Resources, pp. 147-149), and the Institute for Earth Education has a whole curriculum that inspires reverence while teaching important ecological concepts.

Wonder Walk

The Wonder Walk is done in pairs with a leader and follower who switch roles halfway through the activity. It can be conducted any place where there is a bit of nature. You can do the Wonder Walk with people of all ages. (With elementary students, however, it's important to do this activity with either a small group or a large ratio of adults to children.)

Have the students pair up, and explain the entire activity before you begin. Let them know that the activity should be done in *complete silence.* The leader will be taking her partner on a very special journey to awaken his senses and invite him to meet different aspects of nature. The one being led will have his eyes closed. Firmly holding her partner's arm, the leader brings the follower to whatever she notices in nature and wants to share. Perhaps she sees a particularly beautiful tree. The leader carefully brings her partner to the tree, tilts his head back, and gently taps next to his eye. This is the signal for him to open his eyes and take a look at whatever he's been led to see, in this case the tree from below. The leader gives her partner a few moments to look before tapping his temple again, the signal to close his eyes. To awaken the sense of touch, the leader might place her partner's hands on the bark of the tree. If she hears the sound of a bird, she might gently pull on her partner's earlobe, the signal to listen. Maybe there is a flower nearby. The leader might bring her partner to the flower, touch the back of her partner's knee to signal him to bend and crouch lower, position his head near the flower, and tap the tip of his nose, the signal to smell.

After about seven to ten minutes, you can ring a chime or whistle, the signal for the students to switch roles. When both students in each pair have had a chance to lead and be led, call them back together to discuss the experience.

I've led this activity with people from age four to seventy-four. I've witnessed children who are scared of bugs gaze in awe at a bumblebee covered in pollen buzzing inside a flower. I've heard inner city students gasp in astonished joy as they watched a baby groundhog at a nearby park peak out of his burrow and stare at them. As long as I remind participants to stay completely quiet during the activity, they almost always experience reverence for our mysterious world. Once they've had this experience, it becomes so much more obvious why it's worth protecting our planet. Instead of an intellectual appreciation of environmental preservation, these children have a visceral understanding of what it is they are being asked to protect. They care because they've seen and heard and felt the wonder of this earth.

RESPECT

Respect can be understood as reverence turned from an emotion into an attitude or action. Respect isn't something we simply feel — it's something we show through our words and behaviors. Respect follows naturally on the heels of reverence, but we do not *have* to feel reverence to show respect. Respect also means refraining from interfering with another's rights. Children need to be taught to show respect whether or not they honor or revere someone or something. It is this hands-off respect that is so important for protecting the Earth's resources upon which all life depends, for preventing hate crimes when prejudice exists, or for eliminating cruelty to animals, whether we like them or not. Students may not revere a certain religion, but they ought to be respectful of others' beliefs and not desecrate mosques or synagogues. They may not revere. earthworms, but they ought not to dig them up and cut them in half. There are ways to promote respect without resorting to a litany of rules that forbid trespassing upon others' rights or interests. For example, classes on different religions that bring to light the wisdom and compassion in other belief systems will help students show respect toward others who may appear different from them. A lesson on the ways in which earthworms turn what we consider to be waste into fertile soil can go a long way toward promoting respect, if not reverence, for them.

The humane educator promotes respect by demonstrating respect. No educational approach is more powerful than example, and humane educators teach largely by modeling the message they wish to instill in their students. First, humane educators model respect and compassion for their students. They listen well and treat their students with kindness. They also insist that the students treat each other likewise. Next, humane educators model living with respect and kindness towards others by making humane choices. They also remain open to new information so that they can continually make kinder decisions. In other words, humane educators actively endeavor to make their own lives their message. In so doing, they invite their students to explore living with more respect, too.

To help you examine your own life's message and create goals for better modeling your values, you'll find the *My Life Is My Message* questionnaire (p. 123).

RESPONSIBILITY

When students experience reverence and have been taught and inspired to be respectful, taking responsibility will likely be an inevitable step. Responsibility comes when we acknowledge the role we play in our interconnected relationships with one another, other species, and the environment, and put our respect into practice. If young people learn that their choices matter, and that their individual lives can be an expression of integrity and kindness, they will likely take responsibility for improving their own lives and the world. Humane education does not burden children with the responsibility for changing the world themselves, but rather inspires them to live life responsibly through both their personal choices and their full involvement as engaged citizens.

It is sometimes difficult to recognize the ways in which we are responsible for the problems in our world. Our individual lives may seem so insignificant in the face of enormous challenges such as global warming, species extinction, pollution, slavery, poverty, starvation, or institutionalized animal cruelty. It is especially hard to realize our part in atrocities when others seem to be the obvious culprits. Corporations that pour toxins into waterways, agribusinesses that perpetuate factory farming, governments that oppress their citizens — these appear to be the guilty parties. Many people fail to understand the part they play in causing suffering because their contribution seems so miniscule compared to the power that multinational corporations and governments wield in bringing about and escalating the problems of our time. We can all feel distanced from our role in contributing to suffering even if we are not among the truly disenfranchised. I'm not suggesting that certain corporations, media, or governments are blameless, but it's critical that we each recognize our personal responsibility to live and choose according to our values. At the same time, corporations and governments are all made of people, each of whom can be influenced by new ideas, visions, and attitudes of equity, compassion, and sustainability. If we become aware of problems, we have the responsibility not only to divest ourselves of complicity whenever we can, but also to voice our concerns to executives and elected officials.

One way to help students understand that they are not only the agents of their own lives, but also citizens of the world who share in the responsibility to make our planet safe, healthy, and sustainable is to discuss hypothetical situations. For example, you might describe the scenarios below and ask the class, "What, if anything, should you do in the following situations?"

- You hear about plans to build an incinerator in a low-income neighborhood nearby which threatens to create health hazards for local residents.
- You learn that your favorite cereal comes from a company that was purchased by a tobacco corporation that's promoting tobacco use around the world.
- You find out that the school cafeteria sells food that comes from factory farms where animals are mistreated, and that none of the cafeteria food is organic.

Such hypothetical questions and moral problems engage young people in assessing their own responsibility to solve problems. From the local (the school cafeteria) to the global (a tobacco multinational), students can understand that it takes courage, perseverance, commitment, and integrity to be a responsible and humane citizen.

Element 4: Providing Positive Choices

What makes humane education so effective as a method of positive change is its emphasis on personal choices. Humane educators don't tell students which choices to make, but they teach them that their choices matter. When students examine their consumer choices, they discover that their dollar is a vote on behalf of their values. When they evaluate the impact of a single letter to a legislator on an issue of importance to them, they recognize that their political voice can make a difference.

The Choices Cards described in Chapter One are one way in which humane educators might introduce the concept of positive choices. Another approach is to actually bring in a variety of products for students to analyze and compare. For example, you might fill a canvas bag with various items. As you pull them out from the bag, you can ask your students, "Which is better for you, other people, the environment, and animals?" The students might compare a ceramic mug with a polystyrene cup, a disposable diaper with a cloth diaper, and a commercial window cleaner with a spray bottle containing a mixture of white vinegar and water. The canvas bag itself can be contrasted with a plastic bag from a supermarket. You can ask your students to assess the choices using the following questions:

- Which of these two products lasts longer?
- Which product uses up more resources (taking into account the lifespan of the products)?
- Which of these two products costs less (taking into account the lifespan of the products)?
- Why do so many people choose the costlier, more environmentally destructive product over the reusable product?

The answer to the last question is usually "convenience and ease." It is simply easier to use paper, plastic, or polystyrene when trying to serve a large group of people a meal. Disposable diapers, while costly to the environment and to our pocketbooks, are more convenient than cloth diapers. Sometimes students will recognize how much advertising has influenced their choices. They may have never realized that a mix of vinegar and water cleans windows and counters because make-it-yourself vinegar and water solutions are never advertised on TV. As students explore the reasons they and others make the choices they do, they become more empowered to choose consciously.

Of course, in order to make more humane choices, all of us need access to these choices. It's all well and good to invite students to compare organic, non-genetically-engineered food to conventional, pesticide-sprayed and genetically modified food, but if there are no food co-ops, natural foods stores, or Community Supported Agriculture (CSA) collectives in their neighborhood, or if costs for healthier, more environmentally friendly foods are prohibitive, then one cannot really make different choices. If the school cafeteria only serves unhealthy, high-fat, processed, and nonorganic foods and provides vending machines filled with sugary drinks and candy, it's difficult for the message of healthy choice-making to have meaning.

Often the choice then becomes to use one's voice to initiate change. Students may not have a choice between organic and nonorganic foods in the cafeteria, but they do have a choice about whether they will work together with the school to ensure healthier and more humane food options in the cafeteria. You can help students find ways to create access to more choices in general by having them write letters to the editor of local papers, to store managers, and to legislators, or put together a newsletter for the rest of the school community. Finally, you can dispel the myth that citizens are powerless to effect changes in our society and teach students that their dollar is their loud and powerful vote.

Such activities not only help students practice academic skills such as expressing ideas in a clear, organized way, they also help them realize that they have the power to bring about change.

❖ ❖ ❖

The combination of the Four Elements — providing accurate information, fostering the 3 Cs, instilling the 3 Rs, and offering positive choices — provides the foundation for the development of deeply humane citizens. There is an alchemy involved in humane education. It is not as if each class will always have a balance of all four elements. An entire class might be devoted to a film that inspires compassion and care. Another might be focused solely on developing good critical thinking skills, another to letter writing and using one's voice effectively. But by having the Four Elements as the guiding principle for a humane education unit, course, or curriculum, students will be invited to:

- Care deeply
- Assess critically
- Create freely
- Choose wisely.

THE POWER AND PROMISE OF HUMANE EDUCATION — PROFILE 2: BRIAN

Khalif Williams, the executive director of the International Institute for Humane Education, used to work in a Rochester, NY, residential treatment facility for emotionally disturbed, mentally ill adolescent boys with behavior disorders. Most of these boys had suffered from severe mental, physical and sexual abuse, and had also become perpetrators to various degrees, acting out violently, molesting, verbally assaulting others, and setting fires. Although these traumatized boys were kept somewhat safe at this residential facility and received some nurturing, they almost never had the opportunity to leave the campus where they lived. Living in close quarters with other disturbed, often violent boys, and with counselors monitoring and controlling their actions kept them in a perpetual state of self-defensive vigilance. They were given no opportunities to practice being gentle, compassionate, or receptive.

Khalif began taking some of the boys to a nearby nature reserve to alleviate the pressures of their confined life at school and to expose them to the beauty and interesting wildlife that abounds in the natural world. At the reserve, birds would routinely eat out of one's hands if one stood very still holding out birdseed. For a while, Khalif took the boys to the reserve once a week, and as time went by the few boys who were going to the reserve began talking about their weekly experiences. Some of the more challenging boys who had not been part of the field trips began to show interest. One day Brian decided he wanted to go. Brian had a reputation with the staff and other boys as being unpredictable, violent, prone to dark, disturbing flights of imagination, and delighted by the misfortune of others.

When Brian arrived at the reserve he took his time choosing a spot to begin feeding the birds. He held out his birdseed-filled hands perfectly still for almost 5 minutes (the longest he had been still, except when sleeping, since Khalif had met him a year before). Suddenly Brian was enveloped in a halo of fluttering birds, all seeming to gravitate to him over the others. Khalif drew the boys' attention to Brian, and their jaws dropped.

On the walk back to the van and the subsequent ride home, the vision of Brian surrounded by birds was all the boys could talk about. They were exchanging ideas about how one could be more still, more inviting to the woodland animals, more gentle, an even better "person in the woods." The students shared the story of Brian and the birds numerous times over the following days, casting Brain in a new light — even to himself. He was no longer "Brian who has trouble controlling himself," but "Brian who has problems but can be gentle and intimate with some of the world's most delicate creatures." Brian began to seek out more opportunities to express his gentleness. Soon, other challenging residents were asking to come along on Khalif's outings to the woods, too.

THREE

Humane Education in Practice

"Humane Education offers real hope for the new century."
— David Selby

Elementary Schools

PEDRO COMES FOR A VISIT

A third grade class eagerly awaits their introduction to Pedro. Their teacher has been telling them for a week that Pedro is coming to talk to their class, but she hasn't told them much more. "Who's Pedro?" the students ask, but their teacher is secretive. All she will say is that Pedro is from Central America and that he is anxious to share his story with the students.

It turns out that Pedro is a Panamanian parrot, a puppet to be more precise, and on the morning Pedro is visiting, the teacher has placed him on a low branch on a tree by the school. She leads the class to the tree and asks the students to look up to meet Pedro. Sliding her hand into the puppet, she asks Pedro if he would like to come into the classroom and meet the children.

"Sí, Senora," answers Pedro, and the teacher gently lifts the puppet from the tree and returns to the room, with Pedro squawking the whole way, asking whether there will be delicious fruits and nuts in the school, whether the children will help him, whether they have ever seen such a magnificent bird.

Back in the classroom, Pedro tells the children his story. First he describes the beautiful rainforest where he is from, painting a vivid picture of the lush, wet, life-filled world that is home to parrots and so many other species. He describes the complexity of interdependent life in the forests and explains that half of all species on Earth reside in rainforests. Pedro teaches the children that the rainforests produce oxygen and are home to plants that are used to make medicines. When the image is complete, he tells the children what is happening to the rainforests, how they are being cut down for fancy wood furniture and burned in order to create pasture for cattle grazing and crops. He describes the devastation that follows deforestation, that the soil cannot support crops or grass for very long once the forests have been destroyed and that each second of each day an area of rainforest the size of a football field is destroyed forever.

Then Pedro says, "But that's not all! It's bad enough that our homes are being ruined, but we parrots are scared of something else, too." Pedro goes on to explain how adult parrots are being killed so that their young can be gathered from nests, crammed into boxes, and shipped illegally to other countries (including the United States) where they will be sold as pets. He tells the children that usually about half of the young parrots die before they ever reach a pet store. Then Pedro reveals that he himself watched this happen, but escaped to tell others: "That is why I'm here today, to tell you about what is happening to parrots and to rainforests, so that you can help me and my friends."

The children are invited to ask Pedro questions, and usually someone will ask what they can do to help Pedro and the forest. Pedro gives them many choices. "First," he says, "you can tell your parents about me and together you can avoid buying anything that comes from destroying the rainforests." He explains how some hamburger meat, especially from fast food restaurants, comes from cows grazed on land that was once covered in rainforests: "Usually, the meat is ground up and mixed with meat from your own country and labeled as being from America, so it is difficult to know, but cheap hamburger meat often comes from cattle grazed on destroyed rainforests." He tells them that teak and mahogany are woods that often come from cutting down rainforests, so unless they are clearly labeled as being harvested sustainably, avoiding such wood helps, too. "Of course, I hope you won't buy a parrot to live in a cage in your house! We want our freedom and our forests, just like you want your freedom and your own homes."

Pedro then tells the children the positive things they can do to help. By buying products that come from thriving rainforests, families can help the rainforests to survive and help those people who rely upon the rich gifts of the forests to flourish as well. He also tells them about organizations that are protecting rainforests and helping people farm sustainably, and about children's groups that are raising money to help save rainforests. He asks the teacher to bring out a box of items to show the children — some of which come at the expense of rainforests (like carvings made from rare woods or conventional coffee beans) and some of which come about only through the forests' continued existence (like buttons made from tagua nuts, shade-grown coffee beans, and certain medicines).

Pedro thanks the children for talking to him and for caring about the rainforests and parrots like him. He reminds them that their choices matter, that how they live their own lives makes a difference for others, and asks them to think about other ways in which they can help rainforests and parrots. He also tells them that there is hope for the rainforests and for parrots, which is why he is visiting children and talking to them. "Tell your friends and your parents!" Pedro squawks, as he bids his farewell: "Adios. Muchas gracias!"

❖ ❖ ❖

While it's important not to overwhelm young children with the ills of the world, the suffering people and animals endure, or the frightening scenarios of an environmentally degraded world, it is critical to awaken children's compassion and sense of citizenship, to raise their awareness about changes that they can affect through their own daily choices, to nurture their reverence and respect, and to set the stage for them to take responsibility in age-appropriate ways. Pedro does just that in a lively, fun, and entertaining manner that is serious yet child-friendly.

Humane education can be incorporated into the K-5 curriculum by bringing into the classroom an appreciation for others and an understanding of the interconnections between all of us around the globe. It is not too early to teach elementary-aged children that they vote with their dollars and their choices, nor to introduce them to the ways in which television and other media influence them to want certain products. Media literacy can begin quite young — after all, young people are the targets of ad campaigns that rely on children's naiveté for success. Even students in the early years of elementary school can learn to assess information carefully.

Ideally, humane education would begin in kindergarten. Classroom teachers and homeschooling parents would foster children's reverence, ignite their compassion, and introduce them to the power of conscious citizenship. They would take field trips to parks and gardens, plant herbs and vegetables, raise money for worthy causes, listen to tales of characters with character, practice stewardship in their classroom and home as well as respect for their classmates, teachers, and family. As they moved up the grades, teachers would share stories of great leaders and saints — people like Martin Luther King Jr., Mahatma Gandhi, and Mother Theresa — and begin to explore issues of prejudice so they would be able to rise to the challenge of eradicating various forms of hatred in themselves and in their classrooms. Teachers would also examine moral dilemmas with their students so that the children could use their own best creative and critical thinking skills to come up with solutions. For example, a fourth grade teacher might share the following scenarios and ask the class to respond with ideas about how to solve the problems:

Scenario 1: Jeremy, a nine-year-old boy, has witnessed two friends stealing from a local store. Jeremy doesn't want to tell on his friends, but he knows that what they have done is wrong. What should Jeremy do?

Scenario 2: Ten-year-old Maria is sitting with her friends at lunch when they start talking about a girl in their class in a mean way. They plan to play a trick on the girl that is hurtful. What should Maria do?

Scenario 3: Henry's fourth grade class has a spelling test, and Henry finds himself peeking at his neighbor's work because he did not study for the test. When he gets his test back, he's gotten 100%. Henry starts cheating on every test. Charlie, Henry's best friend, sees Henry cheat one day. What should Charlie do? Sam, who isn't friends with Henry, sees him cheat. What should Sam do?

These scenarios are tough, asking children to balance friendship and loyalty with integrity and honesty. While these imaginary scenes focus on interpersonal rights and wrongs, they pave the way for children to grapple with global issues as they get older. There are other scenarios that focus on humane issues that elementary aged children can explore, too, such as the following:

Companion animals: Nine-year-old Sarah wants a dog, and Sarah's parents are excited to bring a dog into their home, but they want a golden retriever puppy because they believe that this breed is good with children, and they also feel that it's better to purchase a puppy than to adopt an older dog who may have behavioral problems. Sarah has learned about dog overpopulation in school, and she knows that there are dogs at shelters who desperately need good homes. Sarah doesn't want her family to contribute to the overpopulation problem by purchasing a purebred dog from a breeder, but she wants to have a good dog, too. What should Sarah do? (Your local SPCA or Humane Society will likely be able to provide a speaker, lesson plans, and/or a visit to the shelter to supply further information for assessing issues related to companion animals.)

Sweatshop workers: Mark wants new clothes for school. He's tired of wearing hand-me-downs and especially wants new basketball shoes, along with regular sneakers. His parents don't have much money, so in order to get new clothes and shoes, they shop at a discount chain store. But Mark has learned that these stores sell clothes that are often produced by people in sweatshops, and he doesn't want some kid to have suffered in a factory so that he can have new stuff. What should Mark do? (For further information about clothes, brands, and fair trade, see pp. 138-139.)

Scenarios such as these bring out contradictions between our desires and ethics, and they do not lend themselves to superficial thinking. They require students to be creative in finding good solutions. Teachers can raise these issues with students and enlist their minds and hearts in coming up with ideas for balancing personal wishes with kindness toward others. Even young students can begin to explore such issues and examine their own values. Before embarking on these questions and issues, however, it's important to enlist the support of parents and school administrators, so that you are not presenting issues that conflict with a particular family's values. Discussions with the school counselor about student readiness to assess personal choices in light of new information will also help ensure that the scenarios and issues you discuss are appropriate.

Secondary Schools

In junior high and high school, teachers can expose their students to the complexity of humane education issues and provide the varied and sometimes disturbing information necessary to work toward truly humane solutions to worldwide problems. Preferably, humane education would be taught as its own subject, but it can also be incorporated into the existing curricula (see pp. 118-121 for more information about infusing the standard curricula with humane education). Teachers who wish to incorporate humane education into their subjects, however, need to take care not to create a piecemeal approach that fails to achieve the real potential of a better thought-out curriculum.

It would be a mistake to dismiss the effort to implement widespread humane education courses at the secondary school level as impractical given limited funds and faculty, the growing number of unfunded mandates, an already overburdened infrastructure, and the current emphasis on standards-based tests. Humane education offers such enormous benefits to individual students, the greater society, other species, and the environment that it would be unwise not to make room for this powerful field of study despite the obstacles.

In my experience, secondary school students who are exposed to humane education:

- Are less susceptible to media messages
- Become better critical thinkers
- Develop more compassionate attitudes towards others
- Take more responsibility for their actions and choices
- Gain lifelong problem-solving skills
- Often have increased self-confidence and self-respect
- Become more conscious of their duties as citizens
- Demonstrate leadership qualities and skills
- Are empowered to be agents of positive change
- Actually improve the world.

The following activity provides insight into how the benefits above might be realized through a humane education activity:

MANY COLORS

Many Colors was originally based upon the conflict that ensued between environmentalists and loggers when the Northern Spotted Owl was threatened with extinction because of logging in the Pacific Northwest. Loggers and environmentalists were at odds, and the media reported on the issue only in either/or terms: *either* loggers have jobs and the spotted owls die *or* loggers lose their livelihoods and spotted owls survive. This either-or thinking encouraged people to take sides rather than look for solutions to the problem. Many Colors invites students to actually solve the problem instead of taking sides.

In this activity, teachers divide the class into four groups: loggers, environmentalists, problem-solvers, and citizen choice-makers. The loggers and environmentalists research the issue from their personal perspective and then present their views to the class. The problem-solvers conduct their own research on solutions to the conflict and brainstorm answers to the problem. After hearing from the loggers, environmentalists, and problem-solvers, the citizen choice-makers gather to come up with all the ways in which they as individuals can help implement solutions. (For a detailed description of this activity, see pp. 82.)

At the end of this project, students will have acquired knowledge:

- About an important environmental issue: the protection of endangered species
- About an important social issue: protecting jobs for people.

They will have also learned:
- To listen to different points of view and to think critically about information
- To question information and its source
- To seek out and pursue creative solutions to apparently intractable problems
- To accept individual responsibility for implementing solutions
- To take a leadership role in solving conflicts.

And they will have used all of the Four Elements of humane education in the process.

Such an activity lends itself to investigating a wide variety of controversial topics. You can use this format to study any issue that is, or has been, presented by the media in either-or terms, such as:

- Going to war against Iraq in 2003
- Passing NAFTA and GATT in the 1990s
- Exterminating introduced animals in areas where they threaten indigenous species.

Giving young people the opportunity to fully research an issue of our time and to work toward positive solutions to complex problems is not only empowering, it actually helps to solve these problems as students take on the responsibilities of citizenship.

There is so much at your disposal for conducting humane education classes. Fodder for critical thinking is everywhere. Whether it's corporate curricula sent free to schools (primarily endorsing a corporation or its perspective), industry posters on the hall walls (meant to sell certain products), or simply the food served in the cafeteria, you can easily find materials and topics to discuss.

Imagine a teacher whose school has contracted with Channel 1 to show its daily 12-minute TV program to students. Although billed as a valuable news show for teens, Channel 1 is a for-profit venture that includes commercials. Channel 1 sells its expensive commercial spots to companies promising them a captive audience. The contract stipulates that 90% of the students must watch Channel 1 on 90% of school days, and it requires students to watch the two minutes of Channel 1 commercials as well. Many believe that Channel 1 does not belong in schools, but since the corporation provides free televisions (enabling schools with limited funding to show educational videos), many schools are willing to sign on.

The Channel 1 contract does not prevent teachers from using the show and its commercials as a critical thinking tool to analyze media and advertising, however. If you are a teacher at a school that contracts with Channel 1, you can use the program to help your students become more media savvy rather than showing it simply for its intended purpose (which ultimately is to make money for the corporation that owns Channel 1).

You can also utilize the free curricular materials you may receive from corporations. If McDonald's provides free lesson plans on nutrition, if Proctor and Gamble provide free materials on solid waste, and if chemical and oil companies send free curricula on environmental science, you can ask your students to determine what information is *left out* of the materials. What are students being led to believe through these curricula, and what other information would they need to obtain in order to have a well-rounded knowledge of the issues or subject matter?

A couple of years ago when I was visiting a school, I noticed a United States Department of Agriculture (USDA) poster hanging in the cafeteria. The poster included a picture of an athletic teenager playing basketball surrounded by photos of a pepperoni pizza, whole milk, and a cheeseburger. The text read: "The Healthy School Lunch Program." I remember feeling startled by the poster that seemed to be advertising primarily high fat foods. Obesity among children in the U.S. is epidemic, and heart disease is still the leading cause of death in America, so depicting predominantly high fat foods does not contribute to health. On the contrary, consuming such foods in excess obviously contributes to a host of diseases and conditions. Rather than leave such a poster unexamined, teachers can ask students to analyze and critique it. Students can write letters to the USDA and to the federal school lunch program (which actually distributes high fat foods to schools to help farmers dispose of surplus fatty foods). They can read and evaluate the nutrition information that comes to schools from the dairy council and meat board and contrast it with information that comes from sources without a profit incentive.

While the Internet and books provide a wealth of information, there is nothing like firsthand visits and experiences so that students may bear witness to the realities behind their choices. Since one of humane education's primary goals is to promote informed citizenship and mindful decision-making, it's important that youth learn about the effects of their everyday decisions including:

- What they wear
- What products they use
- What they eat
- What entertainments they pick
- What transportation they utilize
- What treatment they afford themselves, other people, and animals.

Field trips offer powerful learning experiences. By witnessing the behind-the-scenes effects of our choices, we can make more deliberate decisions. When I teach humane education courses, I always try to schedule field trips. Perhaps the most powerful trips I've taken students on have been to modern facilities where animals are raised for food. Because these trips were so eye-opening, I've decided to describe them in some detail below.

Having heard quite a bit about veal production, I called the Pennsylvania Veal Association to request a tour for my students of a modern, intensive veal operation. My request was denied. They did, however, send a video and brochures. I showed these to the students and compared the Veal Association's materials with undercover footage of veal barns. The students and I wrote letters to the Pennsylvania Veal Association again requesting a tour since their video's positive image of veal production stood in stark contrast with the undercover footage we had seen. Three months later I received a call from the owner of a confinement veal facility who invited us to tour her farm. I brought a group of students to this facility. We were not permitted to take photographs or videotape what we saw. Our guides included the owners of the facility, the president of the Pennsylvania Veal Association, a Pennsylvania State University agricultural professor, and a representative from the feed company that supplied the powdered milk that was the only food the calves received during their four-month lives. What we saw confirmed what the students had seen in the undercover footage. The calves were confined in tiny stalls barely bigger than their bodies. They were chained at the neck, unable to turn around or take more than a single step forward or backward.

It was quite an experience for the students to actually see for themselves the conditions under which farmed animals are routinely raised today. The reality was quite different from the storybook images they had in their minds.

I took another group of students to visit a modern egg facility. To arrange this tour, I simply called the county extension office, explained that I was a teacher and wanted to bring a group of students to a modern animal agriculture operation, and was directed to a farm in Lancaster County, Pennsylvania, that housed half a million hens and provided eggs for sale from Maryland to Maine.

When we arrived, the students watched as a non-stop stream of eggs traveled by conveyor to a machine where they were examined under ultraviolet light before being weighed by mechanical arms that placed them in appropriate cartons. We also saw the hens themselves. From floor to ceiling hundreds of thousands of chickens were crammed into tiny, stacked cages, each hen having barely more floor space than the size of this book. The wire floor of the cage sloped so that when a hen laid an egg it would roll down onto the conveyor belt that carried the eggs to the sorting building. The chickens looked awful. Their normally upright, red combs were pink and drooped over their eyes. Many of them were missing feathers and had raw wounds. Each had a blunt, deformed beak because as chicks their beaks were severed to prevent them from pecking each other to death under such confined conditions. The sound was deafening, and the stench was almost overwhelming. Below the tiers of cages was a huge pit, piled high with chicken excrement. When I asked how often the pit was cleaned, our guide said that it was only cleaned out when the chickens were sent to slaughter. This happened after about a year when the hens' bodies were so depleted that they could no longer produce many eggs.

While I could have shown my students video footage of such a facility or photographs of these battery cages, nothing could take the place of actually seeing (and smelling and hearing) it for themselves.

Visiting factory farms, stockyards, or slaughterhouses raises interesting and important questions about our treatment of animals. What are considered normal and legal farming practices (severe confinement, mutilations without anesthesia, branding) would be illegal if they were done to other nonhuman animals. For example, while it's routine to castrate pigs, cows, and sheep without pain relief or anesthesia, it would be illegal with dogs or cats. While billions of chickens are crammed into cages and sheds in the egg and broiler industries, doing this with canaries or parakeets would be illegal under state anti-cruelty laws (which specifically exclude farm animals). And while a man who dumped a litter of puppies into a dumpster was prosecuted for animal cruelty, none of the hatchery owners are prosecuted for routinely throwing male chicks (useless for the egg industry and too small for the broiler industry) into dumpsters. It's rare for teachers to discuss such issues with students, but it shouldn't be. Every day, we contribute to animal suffering through dietary, and other, decisions, yet few of us are aware of the effects of our daily choices on animals. Humane education, unlike other forms of social justice or environmental education, includes the plight of individual animals and invites students to explore our obligations and responsibilities toward them. If I've belabored the issue of animal protection here, it is because animal issues are generally neglected in education, even in sustainability education, environmental education, character education, social justice education, and media literacy education.

As I've said, it is not easy to gain access to places where animals, people, or nature are exploited. However, with a bit of legwork it's possible to schedule informative and meaningful visits to places that provide the background information that is critical to making informed and humane decisions about everyday actions and behaviors. Again, it's important to have the support of parents, school administrators, and counselors before scheduling such visits. Ideally, teachers and parents would be allies in their efforts to educate children to be humane choice-makers, but this is not necessarily the case, and parents must always grant permission for field trips, some of which admittedly, no matter how educational and important, can be upsetting. The same holds for activities in the classroom that might be considered controversial.

VISION INTO PRACTICE

One way to end a humane education presentation is to offer a guided visualization that allows students to imagine the world they want most and to chart their own course toward its realization. You can ask students to close their eyes, sit comfortably, and breathe deeply. Then you might say something like this: "Imagine the world you would most like to live in. What is this world like? How is different from the world we live in today? How do people treat each other?

The earth? Animals? What are people's lives like? What is the natural world like? What are the lives of animals like? Allow yourself to imagine the best possible world you can. And now open your eyes, and take a few minutes to write down your vision of a better world."

After the class has had some time to write, invite them to share their vision of this better world and write their comments and ideas on one side of a black- or whiteboard. When the vision is complete, choose aspects of the new world they've collectively described and ask the students to come up with ideas for how that piece of the vision could become real. Then list these ideas on the other side of the board, until one side of the board is filled with a vision and the other side is filled with ideas for putting it into practice.

Finally, you can ask your students to close their eyes one more time and to consider one small thing that they are willing to commit to doing — or not doing — to help bring about the vision. Stress that they should make a small promise that they can keep, knowing that there is always time to make more promises in the future. Ask them to open their eyes and to share their promise aloud. One by one, students voice their commitments, which are witnessed by their peers. Their words inspire and bring hope to their classmates as they realize that together they can make their visions real.

This is the power and promise of humane education: Young people, equipped with knowledge and compassion, living according to humane values, and making the world a better place for themselves and everyone else.

THE POWER AND PROMISE OF HUMANE EDUCATION PROFILE 3: MIKE

Mike, a very bright high school senior, took an after school humane education course that I taught at his large high school in a Philadelphia suburb. During the course, Mike never cracked a smile or expressed empathy, and he appeared detached from the content of the course. He always listened attentively, but he did not seem to care about the issues we discussed. On the last day of class, a week before he would graduate, he participated in a Council of All Beings (see pp. 104), an activity in which students have the opportunity to become, through their imagination, another being (whether human, animal, plant, or landscape) and to share their thoughts, concerns, and wisdom with the rest of the group. During the Council Mike became the ocean, and speaking as the ocean he raised his voice and addressed the group saying, "My body is crying, and my tears are poison. The life within me is dying, and my heart is broken." I was dumbfounded. Inside this reserved, seemingly apathetic young man resided a poet, who, when all was said and done, actually had come to care very deeply.

Whether it was the fact that he had been stretched in new ways by an unusual mode of learning in the Council of All Beings; whether it was the cumulative effect of a semester's worth of information, or whether it was the influence of other students who had begun to take more responsibility for their choices, Mike had been transformed. When the Council was over, each student made a small promise to do something to help the being for whom he or she had spoken. Mike promised to learn more about ocean ecology and to stop buying overpackaged and disposable products that he didn't need. Then, as everyone was saying goodbye, he said, "Of all the classes I have taken in high school, this is what I'm going to remember."

Part Two

f.a.q.s, activities, and suggestions

FOUR

Frequently Asked Questions about Humane Education

Q: How is humane education different from character and values education?

A: In some ways humane education may seem similar to other educational approaches, such as character or values education. But there are two significant differences. Most character and values education programs focus primarily on relationships between people. A few will include our relationship with the environment and animals (primarily companion animals), but the majority of character education programs focus their attention on people-to-people interactions. Character and values education also tends to leave out the effects of our everyday choices on others far removed from us. While a teacher of character education might explore the effects of stealing, bullying, or some other negative character trait on others, it's less common that character education would examine the effects of our choices in personal care products, food, clothing, or transportation. Yet as we've seen, these daily choices can have far-reaching consequences for others.

Humane education encompasses character and values education in the sense that it asks students to practice such virtues as kindness, compassion, and integrity in their personal interactions, but it also asks them to explore what these virtues really imply in terms of their daily life and their personal choices which affect others outside their families and communities. It asks students to be kind not only to their classmates and neighbors, but to everyone whose lives they affect; to show compassion not only toward their dog or cat, but to all animals; to respect not only their own home, but to respect the Earth as well.

Q: What is the difference between humane education and sustainability education?

A: Like humane education, sustainability education is dedicated to creating a world in which humans live both peacefully and sustainably on the planet. As I see it, the only significant difference between the two educational movements is that humane education also includes our relationships with individuals and promotes choices that diminish the suffering not only of entire ecosystems, species, or communities, but also of individual people and animals. For example, whereas sustainability education would generally not provide classes that looked at the suffering of an animal caught in a leghold trap (as long as the trapping were carried out sustainably, meaning that it would not cause overall harm to the species of trapped animal), humane education would consider the suffering of the individual animal caught in the trap as well.

Q: How can teachers possibly add another subject to their already busy schedules?

A: As noted in other sections of this book (see, for example, pp. 113-121), humane education can be incorporated into the existing curricula in ways that add meaning and depth to the standard subjects without unduly increasing a teacher's workload. However, humane education will achieve its true power and promise when it is also taught as its own subject through mandatory courses. I look forward to the day when schools hire humane educators in the same numbers that they hire math teachers. When that day comes, we will begin to witness a profoundly positive transformation in our world as young people graduate with the tools for truly humane citizenship. We will be on a path toward a society that shows respect and compassion towards all. In the meantime, teachers can certainly offer elective courses and lead after school clubs (see pp. 115). Many teachers who read this book and are excited by the subject and approach will look forward to offering a new course as a high school elective. Such a course could fit into the language arts or social studies curriculum quite easily. Rather than adding to their workload, teachers might be able to offer such an elective to replace an existing class, both refreshing and expanding their teaching repertoire.

Q: What can substitute teachers do to promote humane education?

A: Substitute teachers are in an ideal situation to offer humane education lessons. Substitutes often have a great deal of flexibility in offering classes to their students. Many of the humane education activities described in the next section can be used for a single class or a series of classes.

Q: Are there any schools oriented toward or committed to humane education?

A: A humane education charter school has opened in California and plans are underway to create humane education charter schools in New York, Arizona, and New Mexico. The purpose of these schools is to create a learning environment that promotes humane living in addition to teaching the standard subjects.

For example, students in language arts classes will not only learn to read and write, they will have as their subject matter material that helps them to be kind. Art class can rely on nontoxic and recycled materials; word problems in math can address meaningful issues so that students will not only solve mathematical problems, but potentially societal ones as well. Social studies will address the ways in which our life choices impact others and invite students to creatively develop solutions to global challenges. Environmental studies will provide opportunities to both explore and respond to ecological problems. Science classes will use only humane methods for teaching biology. Children will become media literate, rather than simply media consumers. The cafeteria can provide healthy, primarily organic, humane meals. The students, where possible, can tend school gardens that provide vegetables for school lunches.

These schools will graduate students who are proficient in the 3 Rs of reading, writing, and arithmetic, but who have also fully developed the 3 Rs of reverence, respect, and responsibility. They will understand their role as citizens, and will have been inspired to care about others — human and nonhuman – and the beautiful planet Earth.

Such schools will not simply be places where children learn about the ills of the world and take on the responsibility of solving our collective problems. They will be places where teachers provide opportunities for joy and reverence to abound because these feelings are not only essential to being fully human and humane, they are emotions that light the fire for compassion and action.

Each humane education charter school will be unique, created by teachers, parents, and communities that bring different talents and passions to the project. What they will have in common is a commitment to teaching children to do the least amount of harm and the most good and to graduate students who are not only traditionally well-educated, but who also have the tools, desire, and will to be kind.

Q: How does the humane educator avoid bias?

A: It's important to realize that everyone is biased, and humane educators are without question biased towards kindness and compassion. Humane education has as its goal the creation of a humane world through humane citizenship. Teachers who offer humane education know that their job is *not* to tell students what to think or do, but rather to explore issues in all their complexity, to teach good critical thinking skills, to offer healthy and humane choices, and to let the students come to their own decisions. Choosing to live a humane life is a complex and ongoing process without either-or answers. Compassionate people will differ in the ways in which they interpret the humane life. What humane education does is invite students to go on the journey equipped with solid information, the sustaining values of respect and kindness, and excellent skills for decision-making.

Q: How can I become trained in humane education?

A: As I write this book, there are only a few places where one can pursue academic training in broad-based humane education. The organization I co-founded, The International Institute for Humane Education (IIHE), launched the first Humane Education Certificate Program (HECP) in the United States and later affiliated itself with Cambridge College to offer the first Master of Education degree program in Humane Education in the U.S. These distance-learning programs train people to be humane educators who can offer comprehensive humane education primarily at the secondary school level. As of this writing our master's program is the only humane education degree program that includes human rights, animal protection, environmental preservation, and cultural issues in the curriculum.

IIHE also offers weekend *Sowing Seeds* humane education training workshops around the U.S. and Canada. In addition, our faculty, associates, and students lead sessions on humane education at a variety of conferences and community events.

Some people will find that they are able to create their own focus in schools of education that includes humane education, or that they can pursue environmental education, sustainability education, or character education at universities, individualizing their courses and majors to cover humane education.

Schools of education will undoubtedly begin adding humane education courses. Eventually, as humane education becomes more commonplace, I believe all schools of education will provide training and instruction in humane education.

Q: Who pursues training in humane education?

A: In general there are three categories of people who pursue training in humane education:

1. *Activists* who perceive education as one of the most effective ways to create a better world
2. *Teachers* who want to bring humane education into their existing curricula and courses, and
3. *Educational reformers* who want to initiate humane education programs, charter schools, and legislation to make humane education commonplace.

Q: How can I find a humane educator to come to my (or my child's) classroom?

A: There are people trained in the kinds of humane education approaches described in this book in virtually every state and province in the U.S. and Canada.

To find an updated list of websites and email addresses for humane educators, visit IIHE's website at <www.IIHEd.org>.

Q: Shouldn't parents, rather than teachers, be responsible for instilling important values in their children?

A: Humane education promotes values that we all agree are good, such as kindness, compassion, respect, integrity, honesty, and courage. Humane educators help students interpret these values in their daily lives and through their choices. This is definitely a job for schools because the information we need to apply our common values in real life situations is complex and requires research, analysis, and good critical thinking skills — all part and parcel of learning. As long as humane educators do not tell students what choices they should make, but rather give them the tools and empower them to be conscious and informed citizens, they are not supplanting the role of parents.

Humane education in schools will actually reinforce the efforts that parents are making at home. I hope that parents become involved in humane education both at home and in a supporting role in schools. My book *Above All, Be Kind: Raising a Humane Child in Challenging Times* makes the point that once humane education is common, it will be easier for parents to promote humane choice-making at home. At the same time, when parents become their children's humane educators outside of the classroom, the job of teachers gets easier as well.

FIVE

Humane Education Activities

Throughout this book, I have referred to numerous humane education activities. This section provides the details for you to use them yourself. You can modify most of the following lessons by grade and offer them as either a short activity or a longer research project. A visiting humane educator or substitute teacher can use the majority of these activities in a single class period. A classroom teacher might turn the same activity into an ongoing class project. Be creative with these activities. They are offered here to get you started and to inspire your own creativity and imagination, not to become codified as *the* humane education lesson plans.

ALIEN IN THE ETHICAL UNIVERSE

Grades: 5 through 8
Time: 20-45 minutes
Materials: Alien question sheets
Relevant Subjects: Language Arts, Social Studies, and History

When I do this activity, I pretend that I have a friend who is traveling through the universe on a fact-finding mission in order to learn how different beings behave on different planets. She is visiting Earth, and I've brought her with me to talk to the students because she loves asking young people their views since they tend to be very forthright and honest with her. I explain that on her planet all beings are treated equally, with respect and compassion, and that she wants to know the rules on planet Earth so she won't offend anyone. I also explain that because her planet is so far away, she travels in the form of energy and will occupy my body to speak to the students. I ask if the class is willing to answer her questions and close my eyes to let her "enter my body" — and when I open my eyes, it is the alien who addresses the class.

Another way to conduct this activity is to divide the class into groups of five, to ask one member of the group to play the alien who will ask a series of questions to the others in the group, and to record the answers on a piece of paper.

Each subject question has four parts:

1. How are you supposed to treat _____?

2. Is it ever okay to harm _____?

3. Why or why not?

4. Do people generally treat _____ respectfully?

In relation to *humans*, your list can include:

- people with a different skin color

- elderly people

- men/women

- people with disabilities

- people with a different religion

- people who are mentally ill

- people who are poor/people who are rich and powerful

- short people/tall people/fat people/skinny people

- people with brown eyes/blue eyes/hazel eyes/green eyes/pink eyes

and so on.

In relation to *animals*, your list can include:

- animals in general

- birds in general/specific birds such as sparrows, eagles, or chickens

- mammals in general/specific mammals such as dogs, cats, pigs, horses, or coyotes

- fishes

- reptiles

- amphibians

- insects

and so on.

Most of the time, students express the view that we should treat others with respect, but as the "alien" delves deeper, prejudices such as racism, sexism, jingoism, etc. come to light. In relation to animals, the discussion will bring out the inconsistencies between our treatment of different species.

When the students have completed the question-and-answer segment, facilitate a discussion about the inconsistencies, complexities, and confusing aspects of our behaviors and morals. Why do we profess certain values but do not always act accordingly? This discussion about the inconsistencies of our values and actions is the purpose of the activity and sets the stage for further activities that help students put their values into practice more consistently in their day-to-day lives.

JUDGE NOT, LEST YE BE JUDGED

Grades: 7 and up
Time: 20-30 minutes
Materials: A variety of clothing, jewelry, wigs (see below) or photographs of various people
Relevant Subjects: Social Studies and Language Arts
Note: This activity can be done in different ways: it can be teacher-led, student-led, or done with the use of photographs.

Teacher-led version

1. Come into class in your normal clothes and with your normal hairstyle. Tell the class you will be stepping out of the room and when you return they should look at you and immediately write down their feelings, impressions, and thoughts based solely on your appearance. Leave the room and come back wearing a white lab coat (or one of the other costumes listed below). Give the students a minute to write down their impressions and leave again. You can come back wearing any of the following:

- dreadlocks

- a nose ring or lip ring

- a suit jacket

- ragged, dirty clothes

- a Muslim head covering for a woman/turban for a man

- a yarmulke

- a spiked, colored wig

- jewelry, carrying a Tiffany's shopping bag

- glasses (if you don't already wear them)

and so on.

2. Open for discussion. Invite students to share what they wrote, and discuss how stereotypes and prejudices (pre-judgments) limit our openness and receptivity to others.

Student-led version
1. Hand out a bag to each student that has some costume element in it (see above list). In turn, have each student put the item on and have the other students write down their immediate impressions.

2. Follow-up with the same discussion.

Mix and Match
If you are leading this activity by dressing in costumes yourself, mix and match what you've brought (e.g., wear the dreadlocks with the suit jacket or the dirty, ragged clothing while carrying the Tiffany's bag). If the students are wearing the costumes, have them mix and match. Discuss what happens when we are confronted with people who defy our stereotypes.

Photographic version
1. Pass out photographs, and have each student write an immediate impression of the person in the photo.

Photos might include a picture of a:

- Hasidic Jew

- Muslin woman in full head and body covering

- young, black man with knit cap, not smiling

- young, black man in designer clothes, smiling

- obese white woman

- skinny white teenage girl in designer clothes

- person with missing teeth

- white middle-aged man in suit

- person in a wheelchair

and so on.

2. When all the photos have been passed around, ask the students if they imagine details about the person in the photo (e.g., assumptions about the person based solely on their physical appearance in the photograph), and, if so, to write these details on a piece of paper. Collect these comments and the photos and *randomly* attach a page of student comments to a photograph. Pass the photos out again with the randomly attached comments and have students read aloud the comments while showing the photograph to the class. Could the comments be true for the accompanying photograph even though they were probably not written about this photo? Do we really know anything about people based on our stereotypes? Open for discussion. Ask students what they learned about themselves from the exercise, and how it would feel to be stereotyped based on their physical appearance alone.

BE A CRITIC

Grades: 6 and up
Time: 30-45 minutes
Materials: Any printed material
Relevant Subjects: Social Studies, Language Arts, Health, and Science

Professor Wayne Bartz has come up with a method to teach students to be critical thinkers. The acronym for the method is C.R.I.T.I.C., which stands for: Claim? Role of claimant? Information backing the claim? Test? Independent testing? Cause proposed? By using the questions in this acronym to analyze printed material in class, students will be able to bring critical thinking skills to all information they receive.

1. Divide students into groups of four or five and give each group a single piece of printed material (such as an advertisement, a pamphlet from an organization, company, or the government, a poster from an industry or nonprofit group). Ideally, hand out items that contradict one another, so that one group might have a pamphlet that makes a strong case for a position, and another group would have a pamphlet that makes the opposite case.

2. Introduce the C.R.I.T.I.C. questions, and demonstrate how to ask these questions about an item. For example, if you've distributed an ad that claims that a particular diet is healthy and leads to weight loss, you can ask: What is the claim? (Their diet is healthy and leads to weight loss.) What is the role of the claimant? (Their role is to sell the diet to the public.) What information backs up the claim? (Perhaps there are before-and-after pictures of someone

who went on the diet.) Was any test to prove the claim conducted? (The ad might claim that 90% of people on their diet succeed in losing weight.) Was any independent testing conducted? (The ad may or may not have this information.) What is the cause for the weight loss? (The ad may or may not say this.)

3. Have students analyze their printed item, asking the C.R.I.T.I.C. questions.

4. Ask one student from each group to present their analysis to the class and have students discuss whether the ad, pamphlet, article, etc. proves its position and perspective or not.

5. Discuss any contradictory positions.

6. Open for discussion about what students learned from the activity.

BEHIND THE SCENES

Grades: 6 and up
Time: 45 minutes to several weeks, depending upon the detail, research, and involvement of the students
Materials: Items for analysis (see below)
Relevant Subjects: Social Studies, Science, History, Health, Language Arts, and, with modifications, Mathematics.

1. Pick any ordinary product, for example a CD, a bottle of shampoo, a computer, or a T-shirt and ask the class to go backwards in time to determine all the events that had to take place in order for the production and distribution of the product to become possible. To make the lesson even more pertinent to the students and to engage their interest right from the start, you might ask them to pick an item from their desk, their back pack, or clothing for a bit of sleuthing and investigating. Another approach might be to wrap a few items up as gifts, divide the class into groups of five, and give a gift to each group. When the students open the gift, they find not only the item for analysis, but also a list of questions.

Let's say that you choose a conventional T-shirt. The questions accompanying the T-shirt could include the following:

- How did I come into existence?
- Who has been involved in my production?
- Who or what was harmed for me to get to you right now?
- Who or what was helped for me to get to you right now?

2. Have students list everything they can think of that contributed to the production of the T-shirt. This might include

cutting down forests for cropland, planting cotton, applying pesticide, using laborers or machinery to pick the cotton, clean the cotton, and spin the cotton, dyeing, weaving, sewing (and the laborers and machinery involved in these processes), behind-the-scenes factors that enable the machinery and the factories to exist, trucking, distributing the T-shirt, marketing, advertising, transporting it to a store (or a warehouse), using personal transportation to buy the T-shirt, and so on.

3. Once the list is complete, you can move on to another group's or student's product (for the shorter, more limited, version) or, for a longer, more detailed version, extend the analysis. Have each student or each group choose one aspect of the behind-the-scenes factors to research and write a concise description detailing the aspect they've studied. Ask them to include in their report the effects their small part of the big picture of T-shirt production has on people, the environment, and animals. Photocopy these pages and put them together (in a roughly chronological order) so that each student can read a full behind-the-scenes account of the product. (Two excellent resources for this activity are *Stuff: The Secret Lives of Everyday Things* by John C. Ryan and Alan Thein Durning, and the National Science Teachers Association Press publication *The Life Cycle of Everyday Stuff.*)

4. Have students suggest ways in which the production of a T-shirt could be less harmful. For example, the T-shirt could be made using organically grown cotton, no chlorine bleach, and nontoxic dyes, and it could be produced closer to the source of the cotton to minimize transportation. The T-shirt could be sewn by people paid a fair wage and sold by companies committed to selling environmentally and worker-friendly products.

5. Conclusion: Ask students to estimate how many T-shirts (or other products that have been analyzed) they have, and how many they actually wear or use. Did they ever buy a T-shirt (or other product) that they never wear or use? How many do they actually need? Lastly, ask students to consider their own purchasing habits to determine which and how many T-shirts (or other products) they themselves will buy, or not buy, in the future.

TRUE PRICE

Grades: 6 and up
Time: 20-60 minutes
Materials: Items for analysis (see below)
Relevant Subjects: Social Studies, Language Arts, History, Health, Science, and, with modifications, Mathematics

1. True Price offers another way to analyze products. Bring in a variety of products, such as a can of Coke, a wool sweater, a container of ammonia, or a fast food hamburger (or a facsimile of one, available from science/nutrition supply companies).

2. Write several questions on the board:
a) What is the effect of this product on
 • you?
 • other people?
 • animals?
 • the environment?
b) Is the product a want or a need?
c) Was the product available 100 years ago, and, if not, what did people use instead?
d) What else could people use today?

3. If you want the activity to be short, choose a couple of products and assess them during the class, writing down answers to the questions above based on what students and you already know. Discuss what information you would need to have to fully assess the product's true price, that is, its effects on you, other people, animals, and the environment. For a longer version, have students research and analyze an item as a homework assignment and then report about their product to the whole class.

4. Discuss how analyzing items in this way can help people become more conscious consumers. Invite students to consider how willing they are to think about their choices, using the criteria developed during this activity.

TRASH INVESTIGATORS

Grades: 4 and up
Time: 30 minutes
Materials: A garbage can filled with trash items, latex gloves
Relevant Subjects: Social Studies and, with modifications, Science and Mathematics

1. Choose a trash can to analyze (it could be from the cafeteria, hallway, school office, or a classroom). At the end of a day, before the trash is dumped by the school custodian, bring it to your classroom and secure it with a note that it should not be emptied so that you will have a day's worth of trash to analyze the next day.

2. Show the students the can full of trash. Then spread newspaper or plastic on your desk or floor and dump out the entire contents of the trash. Divide the class into groups, and have several students come up and choose an item for their group. If there are enough pieces of garbage for each student, then have every student take an item. Provide latex gloves if necessary.

3. Have students analyze their item by answering the following questions:
- Could this item have been recycled instead of thrown in the trash?

- Could this item have been composted instead of thrown in the trash?

- Could it have been prevented from ever entering the waste stream?

- Is this item a want or a need?

- Could this item have been reused in some creative way instead of thrown in the trash? If so, how? (This is the fun part of this activity. Encourage students to think imaginatively about what else the item could have been used for. They will likely come up with some unusual ideas!)

4. Have students report on their items. If their item was not recyclable, compostable, or reusable in some creative way, have them return the item to the trash can. When all the students have reported, have them look in the trash can again. How do the contents of this trash can compare to its original contents?

5. Conclusion: Facilitate a discussion about waste, resource use, landfills, incinerators, etc. and invite students to consider if and how they might reduce their own trash production.

6. Follow-up: Have students do this activity at home for a week, and plan a visit to your local landfill, incinerator, recycling center, or transfer station.

ANALYZING ADVERTISING

Grades: 5 and up (modify for different ages)
Time: 45-60 minutes
Materials: 1) Poster board (scrap poster board is usually available free from frame shops) with advertising slogans written on one side and enlarged first letters or logos from company names on the other. 2) A variety of print ads aimed at your students' age group. (Alternatively, videotaped copies of television commercials.)
Relevant Subjects: Social Studies and Language Arts

To illustrate the pervasiveness of advertising in your students' lives, "test" their advertising knowledge by holding up a poster you've composed that has familiar advertising slogans written on it. Have each slogan be missing a word. Ask your students to supply the missing word (e.g., "Got ____?" Answer: milk). On the other side of the poster tape enlarged letters from products, such as the "M" from McDonald's, the "G" from the Gap, and the "C" from Crest as well as company logos. Show your students this side of the poster and have them shout out the product/company names just from seeing a single letter or logo.

1. Ask students to consider which ads have influenced them to want specific products. Invite them to be very honest with themselves as they reflect upon advertising's impact on their desires. (They may consider radio, TV, or print advertising.)

2. Spread advertisements from popular and teen magazines over the floor of the classroom. Demonstrate how to analyze the messages embedded in them, using the following questions:

a) What product or service is the ad selling?

b) What deep need or desire is the ad appealing to? (In other words, does the ad appeal to your desire to have love, happiness, wealth, beauty, friendship, joy, etc.?)

c) Who is the intended audience, and what do you suppose their reaction to the ad might be?

d) Who is excluded by the ad (i.e., what classes, races, body types)?

e) What suffering, exploitation, or destruction is hidden from view? (In other words, what suffering of people or animals does the production of the product or the generation of the service lead to and/or what destruction to the environment does the product or service cause?)

f) How does the ad affect your personal desires, self-image, beliefs, and consumer choices?

g) What would life be like without the product or service the ad is selling?

3. Organize groups of four or five students and distribute a small stack of ads to each group. Ask each group to analyze several ads, using the questions above.

4. Have each group report on one of the ads to the class.

5. Facilitate a discussion about how students perceive advertising in a different light now that they've done the exercise, and how their critical thinking skills might enable them to resist advertising messages.

Alternative 1: This activity can also be conducted using videotapes of television commercials. For elementary-age children, videotape the commercials during children's programming (e.g., Saturday morning cartoons). For teens, videotape the commercials during shows that appeal to their age group. Show the commercials during class and analyze them in the same ways as print ads. In addition, have students note the speed with which the images in the commercials change and discuss the effects of this technique with them.

Alternative 2: Have students bring in their favorite ads from home and analyze these instead. Refer to their own preferences in discussions of the ways that advertising targets specific genders, races, age groups and classes of people.

MANY COLORS

Grades: 7 and up
Time: 45 minutes to several weeks, depending upon the amount of research assigned
Materials: For a short version, prepared issue dichotomies with pertinent articles
Relevant Subjects: Social Studies, History, and Language Arts

1. Choose an issue or current conflict that the media and politicians have presented in essentially black-and-white terms. For example,

- loggers versus spotted owls (see pp. 43-44)

- going to war in Iraq in 2003

- passing NAFTA and GATT in the 1990s.

2. Divide the class into four groups representing the two opposing interests (groups 1 and 2), problem-solvers (group 3) and citizen choice-makers (group 4).

3. Have groups 1 and 2 research the issue from their group's assigned perspective. For a short version, have the students read articles that you provide. For a longer version, have groups 1 and 2 search out information as homework and prepare a presentation to the class. Have the group select one person to present its perspective. This student may use photographs, video footage, interviews, personal stories, facts, news reports, statistics — in essence anything that will bolster the group's case.

4. Toss a coin to determine who will go first, and then have each group present its case in turn. Invite members

of groups 3 and 4, the problem-solvers and citizen choice-makers, to ask any questions of groups 1 and 2.

5. During the next phase of the activity, have group 3, the problem-solvers, either suggest alternative solutions (in the short version) or conduct their own research into solutions to the conflict (the longer version). After gathering information, have the problem-solvers brainstorm solutions to the problem. Encourage group 3 to come up with their own ideas, to think creatively, and to consider both large, systemic changes and small, incremental ones. Ask group 3 to anticipate questions and concerns about their ideas and to prepare well thought-out responses. Have group 3 select someone to present its suggestions to the class.

6. When the problem-solvers present their suggestions, encourage members of groups 1, 2 and 4 to ask questions about the implementation of the ideas presented by group 3. Invite groups 1 and 2 to respond to the suggested solutions and to express their thoughts and feelings about the answers group 3 has come up with.

7. Having listened to groups 1, 2 and 3, group 4 should come up with all the ways in which they as individuals and citizen choice-makers can help implement the ideas presented by group 3. These ideas can include writing an op-ed, contacting their legislators, using their money to cast a personal "vote," organizing educational initiatives — in short, activism and advocacy of all kinds. Have members of group 4 implement some of these ideas as their assignment. Ask group 4 to choose someone to present their citizen actions to the class. Again, invite groups 1 and 2 to respond and express their thoughts and feelings about the ideas presented by group 4.

8. Conclusion: Discuss the ways in which a problem can be solved when people come together, listen to each other, and envision creative solutions to conflicts. Invite students to consider how this approach could be applied to other problems.

GREATEST IMPACT

Grades: 9 and up
Time: Several weeks to a month, depending upon the detail, research, and involvement of the students
Materials: Books, periodicals, Internet access
Relevant Subjects: Social Studies, Language Arts, Science, History, and, with modifications, Mathematics

1. Explain that students will be analyzing behaviors and product choices to determine which choices have the biggest impact on the environment, on human health and well-being, and on other species.

2. Write the following personal choices on the board:
   a) Using a highly fuel-efficient car that gets 65 miles per gallon of gas (23 km/liter) or using an SUV that gets 15 miles per gallon (5 km/liter).
   b) Eating a completely vegetarian, whole foods, organic diet or eating the typical American diet (nonorganic, processed and packaged, including regular meals at fast food restaurants).
   c) Buying primarily what you need, usually from second-hand shops or yard sales, or buying approximately twenty new items per week (made with various materials, including petroleum products, wood products, agricultural products, and metal products) that are wants as opposed to needs.
   d) Recycling all paper, plastic, glass and metal or disposing of these in the trash.
   e) Avoiding all disposable and overpackaged products or purchasing products without regard to their packaging and lifespan.

f) Any other lifestyle and product choices you think of that people make regularly.

3. Divide students into groups, with each group attempting to determine the impact of a single choice. Students can assess the impact of these choices by reading books (Mathis Wackernagel and William Rees' *Ecological Footprint* is a very useful resource for this purpose), conducting interviews, doing Internet searches and then writing down the impacts on the environment, human health, and other species.

4. Have each group report on the impact of their choice in the class.

5. Have students assess which choices have the greatest impact and have them rank the choices in order of their greatest positive effect.

6. Open for discussion about which choices are easiest and most difficult to make; which choices can be made independently and which require the cooperation of others (family, schools, community, businesses); which choices can be made by degrees and which have long-term consequences (e.g., one can choose more plant-based foods by degrees, while the choice of a vehicle has long-lasting effects that can't be undone by a different choice the next day).

7. Finally, given the students' research and reporting, have them discuss which choices they will likely make.

WHALE'S STOMACH

Grades: 4 and up
Time: 15-45 minutes
Materials: 1 plastic garbage bag containing 1 plastic one-gallon jug and the remnants of another, 1 trawl net float, 35 feet of nylon rope, 1 large garbage bag, 1 large blob of rubber, 10 small plastic items (e.g., plastic cups, plates, utensils, soda bottle, clear plastic bag, any other plastic containers)
Relevant subjects: Science, Language Arts, and Social Studies

Pertinent information: The bag of items represents the contents of a dying, 28-foot female sperm whale found on a beach in North Carolina in December, 1992. Veterinarians concluded that none but the smallest pieces of plastic could have passed through the whale's intestinal tract, and that the garbage was a large contributing factor to, if not the entire reason for, the whale's death. It is assumed that sperm whales either mistake plastic for food or, perhaps more likely, go after squid that are hiding in and around the garbage and accidentally swallow the plastic as well. Finding plastic in whales is uncommon, but this is not an isolated incident. Most whales who die do so off shore and are not found by people.

1. Stand in front of the class or on your desk and dump the contents of the bag out on the floor of the classroom.

2. Ask students what they think these items have in common.

3. Reveal to the students that a similar collection of items was found in the stomach of a whale who washed up on a North Carolina beach.

4. Have students come up and take an item from the floor back to their desk. If there are not enough items for each student, have the students divide into groups and have a member of each group retrieve an item.

5. Have students examine their item asking the following questions:

- Is this item recyclable or reusable so that it could have been kept out of the waste stream?

- What creative ideas can they come up with to reuse the item?

- How could people have prevented these items from winding up in the ocean?

6. Ask each student (or a member of each group) to report on their item to the whole class.

7. Open for class discussion on how we can diminish the trash we produce and how we can dispose of it responsibly.

WHAT IS A HUMANE LIFE?

Grades: 5 and up
Time: 90-120 minutes
Materials: 1) Mat board or poster board (scraps are available free from most frame shops) with pertinent statistics and facts written on them 2) Props and products that you use in your daily life, plus containers from products (available at local recycling center) you don't use, *or* (for teachers asking for assistance in creating a humane life) a variety of products, some more humane and sustainable than others
Relevant Subjects: Social Studies, Language Arts, Science, and, with modifications, Mathematics

This lively and interactive class can be offered in two different ways. In the first — **Humane Presenter** or **HP** — the teacher models a day in her or his own life as a representative of people consciously trying to live a humane and sustainable lifestyle. This approach works well for visiting humane educators and substitute teachers who are offering a single presentation to the students. In the alternative approach — **Humane Wannabe** or **HW** — the teacher represents someone who would like to lead a more humane and sustainable life but does not know how to and is relying upon the students to provide suggestions and counsel.

Note: If you are going to present this program modeling your own life, it is essential that you accurately share *your* lifestyle, not the lifestyle of the most humane person you can imagine, or the person you want to be in five years (or who you were five years ago). Your honesty and efforts to grow and change, and to live more compassionately and sustainably, are important elements in the integrity of this presentation.

1. Invite the class to join you for a typical Saturday. In the **HP** version, ask the students to think about what the word *humane* means to them (tell them that the word literally means "having what are considered the best qualities of human beings"), and explain that your day reflects a way of living that has slowly evolved for you as you have learned all the ways that your lifestyle choices affect other species, your own health, other people, and the earth. Explain that you try to live a life that harms others as little as possible and that you are continually changing and growing. You might want to tell the students that if you had done this program five years ago, it might have been less humane, and that if you were to do it in five years, you hope it would be even more humane and sustainable. Ask the students to constantly be thinking about the reasons you've chosen certain products or made certain lifestyle decisions and to always ask themselves the following questions:

a) Which is more humane for you, the presenter?
b) Which is more humane for communities of people?
c) Which is more humane for the environment?
d) Which is more humane for other species?

Write these criteria on the blackboard, and throughout the program ask the students whether, in light of the four criteria, an action or product is humane.

In the **HW** version, tell the students that you want to figure out how to lead a more humane life and would like their help. Invite them to suggest choices that are healthier for you and more respectful to other people, other species, and the environment.

2. Pass around facts and statistics. In the **HP** version, provide each student with properly cited facts and statistics that they can read aloud to explain some of your choices. In the **HW** version, provide each student with properly cited facts and statistics that will help them assess your choices and make recommendations to you for living a more humane life. In both versions, invite students to read their statistics or facts to themselves, and remind them to be ready to share them aloud when they are relevant to your typical Saturday. You may want to collect facts and statistics about the following issues (for more information, see the Resources in the back of this book):

- water use
- product testing
- diet and agriculture
- genetic engineering of crops
- sources of pollution
- reasons for habitat destruction
- sweatshop and slave labor use in the manufacture of common products
- fossil fuel and resource use for various activities

3. Begin your day. In the **HP** version, share the products you use in the morning (soap, toothpaste, and so on) in a lively way (for example by taking a mock shower with a shower curtain held by student volunteers and water noises made by the class) and invite students to read aloud pertinent facts or statistics that relate to your choice of products. In the **HW** version, you might describe what you do in the morning (brush your teeth, wash your face), and ask students

to share pertinent facts or statistics. Also ask them to look through the various products you've brought to make recommendations about which ones to use and which ones to avoid.

4. Have breakfast. In the **HP** version, explain, in light of the criteria of humane living, why you have chosen particular foods. Invite students to share pertinent facts and statistics. In the **HW** version, ask students to share relevant facts and statistics and make recommendations about what you might eat, and then perhaps to give you some food in your bowl and a cloth napkin to use (as opposed to the paper napkin that is also one of your props).

5. Other aspects of the day to consider:
   - what to wear
   - how to spend leisure time (e.g., shopping, playing with friends, watching TV, outdoor activities)
   - how to help others (through volunteerism or activism)
   - how to accomplish such chores as house cleaning or laundry in a humane way
   - how to get where you want to go (i.e., what forms of transportation to use)

For each of these topics, have available pertinent objects and materials to choose from (e.g., fair trade, organic clothing and chain store clothing; conventional cleaning products and baking soda and white vinegar) as well as pertinent facts and statistics to help students advise you on your choices. Make your activities as lively as possible!

6. Conclusion: In the **HP** version, invite students to think about their own lives and to consider what changes they

might want to make. Remind them that every humane choice they make matters. In the **HW** version, thank the students for providing suggestions and ideas for making your life more eco-friendly and open for a discussion about how you and they might each begin to make more humane choices now that you all have more information.

CAST YOUR VOTE

Grades: 6 and up
Time: 20-40 minutes
Materials: Pretend money
Relevant Subjects: Social Studies and Language Arts

1. Hand out pretend money to students, giving each person the same amount. Explain that although students cannot vote in elections until they are 18, they vote every time they spend their money. Every dollar they spend is a vote that says, "Do it again!"

2. Place containers for common products on your desk, such as:
   • a box from a name brand athletic shoe
   • the container from a fast food hamburger
   • the wrapping of a common chocolate bar

3. Ask the students if they recognize these items, and if any of them have used, eaten, or purchased similar items.

4. Ask a student to come up and open the shoe box. The student will find the following words written inside: "Ingredients: When you buy this item, in addition to getting the shoes themselves, you contribute to creating jobs for people and to economic growth. But you may also contribute to sweatshop labor, pollution, and animal suffering."

5. Have the student read these words aloud, and ask other students to come and read the "ingredients" inside the other containers as well. For the hamburger, they might read: "When you buy this item, in addition to getting a tasty, convenient meal, you contribute to creating jobs for

people and to economic growth. But you may also contribute to rainforest destruction, species extinction, the
suffering of cows, pesticide use, water waste, pollution,
increases in heart disease, cancer, and obesity, and strip
mall development." For the chocolate bar, they might
read: "When you buy this item, in addition to getting a
delicious dessert, you contribute to creating jobs for people, to economic development, and to world trade. But
you may also contribute to child labor."

6. Once the "hidden ingredients" in the products are read
aloud, explain the connections between the products and
the suffering or destruction they may be causing and ask
students to think of similar products that might not come
with as many hidden ingredients that cause harm (e.g.,
shoes produced locally by people paid a living wage, an
organic veggie burger, fair trade chocolate).

7. Place cans that name product choices on a large shelf
or desk. Include several choices for each product category,
such as:

- second-hand athletic shoes
- sweatshop-free athletic shoes
- conventional new athletic shoes

- a fast food hamburger
- a hamburger made from organic, local beef
- a veggie burger

- a common brand of chocolate bar
- a chocolate bar with "fair trade" and "organic" written on the label
- a piece of fruit.

You can use your imagination and produce many cans for many other items, especially if you have discussed other products in previous activities (e.g., T-shirts or personal care products). Always include at least three choices for each item, for example:

- a conventional new T-shirt
- an organic cotton new T-shirt
- a thrift shop T-shirt

8. Put accurate price tags on each item.

9. Ask students to use their pretend money to "buy" what they would like by coming up and putting their money in the cans they want to "vote" for.

10. Analyze the votes. Which products did students vote for with their dollars, and which ones did they withhold their money from? Why? Which products did they buy despite the fact that the product cost more than a counterpart? Why?

11. Discuss the ramifications of people living their lives conscious of the fact that their dollars are votes. What might change? How might the students spend their money differently after this activity? Ask students how products have already changed because of consumer voting (e.g., the availability of organic foods, the production of hybrid cars and fair trade and cruelty-free products).

12. Conclusion: Explore the ways in which students are and are not inspired to make humane "voting" choices in their own lives.

EXECUTIVE COMMISSION

Grades: 6 and up
Time: 40-60 minutes to a week
Relevant Subjects: Social Studies and Language Arts

This activity can be used in conjunction with any issue that you are discussing, debating, or assessing, from free trade to environmental regulations to genetic engineering of crops to proposed legislation.

1. Pick an issue to debate and create a commission to advise the President/Prime Minister. For example, you might create a commission around this question: Should genetically engineered foods be required to be labeled as such?

2. Divide the class into two equal groups. One group's job is to think of all the reasons in favor of requiring genetically engineered foods to be labeled as such (the "pros"), while the other group's job is to think of all the reasons against creating legislation requiring the labeling of genetically engineered foods (the "cons"). Each group should think of as many reasons as possible (whether or not they personally agree with the reasons), considering such issues as human health and well-being, animal suffering, the environment, and the economy. To turn this into a longer project, have students research the pros and cons as homework before proceeding to the next step.

3. Have a representative from each group list the pros and cons and write these down in two columns on the blackboard. When the lists are complete, ask the students to vote, explaining that they may vote how they truly feel, not based on the group's assignment.

4. Tally the votes and ask the students to write a letter to the President/Prime Minister expressing their opinion on the issue. Put the addresses on the board: The White House, 1600 Pennsylvania Ave., NW, Washington, DC 20500 / Office of the Prime Minister, 80 Wellington Street, Ottawa K1A 0A2. Copy these letters to students' representatives as well. (Letters can also be written to city council members, state/provincial legislators, CEOs of corporations, etc.)

5. When students receive responses from their elected officials, revisit the topic and discuss the role of citizen letters in creating change.

WHAT'S IN A NAME?

Grades: 6 and up
Time: 45 minutes
Materials: Posters with expressions on them (see below)
Relevant Subjects: Social Studies, Language Arts, and Science

Prepare posters with common phrases used to insult people that include animal names, but leave out the animal names. For example:

- Stop eating so much! You're such a _____ (pig).
- He's scared of everything. He's just a _____ (chicken).
- Don't grab all that stuff yourself. You're being a _____ (hog).
- Girls are always talking about others behind their backs. They can be so _____ (catty).
- That old lady is nuts. She's just _____ (batty).
- Her hair is drab, and she's not very noticeable. She's kind of _____ (mousy).
- That woman is always yelling at her husband. She's a _____ (shrew), and he's so _____ (hen-pecked).
- You told on me. You're a _____ (rat).
- That ugly girl! She's a _____ (dog).
- She's fat. What a _____ (cow).
- She's stupid, a real _____ (birdbrain).
- She's hardly touched her food. She eats like a _____ (bird).

1. Discuss the phrases and note that girls and women are more often the object of insults when we use animal metaphors. Ask the class why they think this is the case. Then ask who else is being insulted when we use such phrases —

the animals. When we use this language, who do we think we're insulting? Before you raised this question, were students even aware that they were also insulting animals?

2. Dispel the myths and images about these animals. (For reference and background, I suggest reading Jeffrey Masson's *When Elephants Weep*. For example, birds eat an enormous amount of food for their body weight, while pigs have been *bred* to be huge so that we can have more meat when we slaughter them. Hens will protect their chicks from predators, thus displaying courage, and so on.)

3. Discuss our prejudices against animals. Why do we accord some animals special protections (dogs, cats, and "pet" birds, for example), while depriving equally sentient animals (such as pigs, cows, and chickens) of even minimal protections from cruelty? Ask students what the difference is between a pig and dog or a cow and a cat in terms of their ability to suffer and feel pain. Should we treat all nonhuman animals who are capable of suffering equally? Should they be accorded the same protections from harm as humans? Why or why not?

CHOICES CARDS

Grades: 5 and up
Time: 10-45 minutes, depending upon the number of cards and the approach to analysis
Materials: Cardboard or poster board (scraps are available free from most frame shops)
Relevant Subjects: Social Studies, and, with modifications, Science, Health, and Mathematics

1. To create choices cards, simply consider two related behaviors or products and write one on one side of a piece cardboard/poster board and the other on the reverse. Here are some ideas for cards:

Human Rights:
- shirt from cheap chain store/shirt produced by union workers
- conventional hot chocolate/fair trade hot chocolate
- Rugmart rug/imported rug without the Rugmart (or a similar) label
- volunteering at food pantry/hanging out at the mall
- giving 10% of your allowance to charity/keeping it all
- feeling prejudice/acting on prejudice

Environmental Preservation:
- bottled water/tap water
- hamburger/veggie burger
- disposable diapers/cloth diapers
- organic food/conventional food
- station wagon/SUV
- hybrid car/conventional car
- biking/driving
- buying used clothing/buying new clothing

Animal Protection:
- Cirque de Soleil/Ringling Bros. Circus
- Tom's of Maine toothpaste/Crest toothpaste
- KFC/spaghetti and tomato sauce
- buying a dog/adopting a dog from the shelter
- sport hunting/photographing wildlife
- leather shoes/canvas or hemp shoes
- soy milk/cow's milk

These are just a few examples of choices cards you could make. Use your imagination! The answer to which choice harms less and helps more is sometimes obvious, but some choices cards require knowledge and explanation (e.g., "fair trade," a term applied to products that are produced using fair labor practices; "Rugmart," a label that assures no child or slave labor in the production of the rug; or "Cirque de Soleil," a circus that relies solely upon human performers, not on animal acts).

1. **Short version:** If you don't have much time, you can hold the card in front of the class and read both sides aloud (or ask a student volunteer to do this). Ask the students to determine which choice harms less and helps more, and why. If they don't know, provide background information to enable them to evaluate the choice. Encourage complex thinking and multiple perspectives. For example, some choices may harm one group less but another more.

Long version: Hand out stacks of choices cards to groups of four to five students and ask the groups to discuss their cards and determine which of the two choices on each card harms less and helps more. Ask each group to pick a reporter who will share a couple of the choices with the entire class. Move around from group to group to help explain background information about the choices. Alternatively, give students the opportunity to research information to make decisions about the choices.

2. Conclusion: Invite students to consider what choices they would be willing to make in their own lives to cause more good and less harm to other people, other species, and the ecosystem.

3. Variation: Another option for this activity is to actually bring in objects rather than rely upon the cards. For example, you could bring in an apple with an "Organically grown" sticker and a conventional apple or a chocolate bar with a "fair trade" wrapper and a more commonly available chocolate bar.

WHICH TO PICK?

Grades: 5 and up
Time: 15-30 minutes
Materials: Bag filled with items for comparison (see below)
Relevant Subjects: Social Studies, Science, and, with modifications, Mathematics

Which to Pick? is similar to Choices Cards, but more suitable to an assembly program.

1. Preparation: Gather a variety of similar items that represent a choice between two related objects and put them in a bag. For example, a cloth diaper and a disposable diaper; paper towels and a cloth rag; a polystyrene cup and a ceramic mug; a can of soda and a reusable water bottle; organic, fair trade coffee and conventional coffee; a leather shoe and a canvas or hemp shoe; a plastic shopping bag and the canvas bag you've used to carry all the items; Windex and a spray bottle of white vinegar mixed with water.

2. During an assembly program, bring out your canvas bag and pull out an item, for example the polystyrene cup. Ask students what the item is, how often one might use it, and what one does with it afterwards. When the students say, "Throw it away," toss the cup on the floor. Then pull out the corresponding item, in this case the ceramic mug, and ask students the same questions. Next, ask the students which of the two items harms less and helps more. Lastly, bring out the plastic bag to contrast with the canvas bag. At the end of this activity you will have a large pile of products on the floor — an astonishing display of our "throw it away" lifestyle.

3. Conclusion: Invite students to commit to one small, compassionate choice for people, animals, and the environment.

COUNCIL OF ALL BEINGS

Grades: 4 and up
Time: 1-2 hours
This Council of All Beings is modified from *Thinking Like a Mountain: Toward a Council of All Beings* by Joanna Macy, Arne Naess, John Seed, and Pat Fleming. The book describes a Council that happens over many days, not during a class period. It is possible, however, to do a meaningful short version of this powerful activity.
Materials: 1) A quiet place outdoors or in a room where you won't be disturbed. Avoid rooms with fluorescent lights, or bring a small lamp if you will be doing this activity in a classroom. The mood really does matter in the Council. 2) Art supplies: construction paper, paints, crayons, stones, shells, or other found and recycled objects, scissors, glue, any other art supplies that you have
Relevant Subjects: Social Studies, Language Arts, and, with a follow-up, Science

1. Explain the entire Council before beginning, so that students know what is going to happen. Emphasize that silence (in between the spoken comments of Council members) is an important part of the sanctity of the Council.

2. Invite students to sit or lie down so that they are comfortable. Ask them to close their eyes and let the image of an animal (human or nonhuman), or of a part of nature or landscape, come to them in their imaginations. Remind them not to force themselves to think about a certain animal or part of nature, but rather to let the being visit them in their thoughts.

3. Ask the student to "become" the being that has visited them in their imaginations. Ask that they feel themselves turning into this animal or part of nature (such as a cloud, a mountain, a tree, a wolf, a spider, or another human). Ask them: "What is happening to me as this being? How do I feel? What is my life like? My days? My nights? My interactions with other beings? With my environment? What do I want? What do I have to say? What would I like to tell people? What wisdom do I have as this being?" Remind them to listen inside for the answers.

4. After giving the students some time to really "become" their being, bring the art supplies into the center of the circle and invite the students to open their eyes and *silently* to make a mask to represent themselves as this being. The mask does not have to look like the being as long as it feels like it is representative. Some participants will be tempted to spend a long time on their mask. Remind them that the mask is only a representation, and give a five-minute and a one-minute warning for finishing the mask.

5. When everyone has finished their mask, form the Council.

6. One by one, each being should introduce him-, her-, or itself and say what their life is like, who they are, and how they spend their time. After each being speaks, the Council should respond by saying, "We hear you _____ (name of being)."

7. Ask the beings to each speak again, this time telling the Council what is happening to them, including what people have done to them and what they would like to say to people. Once again, the rest of the group responds by saying "We hear you _____ (name of being)."

8. After each being has spoken again, ask them to talk once more, sharing whatever wisdom, knowledge, or gifts they have to offer, and what they might teach people who are willing to listen. The group responds by saying, "We thank you _____ (name of being)."

9. Finally, after each being has spoken for the last time, ask participants to remove their masks one by one. As each of them takes off the mask, invite them to turn their masks toward themselves and make a small promise to change one aspect of their life that hurts their being.

10. The Council ends when you say something like "These promises made shall not be broken. Many thanks to the beings who have come together today to share their feelings, dreams, hopes, and wisdom."

SCAVENGER HUNT

Grades: All (modify for different ages)
Time: 45-60 minutes
Materials: Scavenger Hunt sheets for each student and an outdoor place to scavenge
Relevant Subjects: Science and, with modifications, Language Arts

This is a special kind of scavenger hunt, different from other ones most of us have participated in as children. In this scavenger hunt, students won't be taking anything; rather they'll be recording their "finds" in a notebook.

1. Explain to students that they will be going on a scavenger hunt, but will not be removing anything. Rather, they will record what they find.
The Hunt:
a) Find five places where you notice interactions between plants and animals.
b) Find three places where human actions have affected the ecology negatively.
c) Find five animals' homes.
d) Find five separate places where the smells are distinctly different.
e) Standing or sitting in one place, with your eyes shut, listen carefully. How many different sounds do you hear?
f) Find three separate places where the temperature is different.
g) Choose a square foot of land, and record how many different life forms are visible.

2. Following the Scavenger Hunt, have students report on their experiences. Additionally, students can write a report or do further investigation into some aspect of the scavenger hunt that inspired them to learn more.

SMELL TEAS

Grades: All (modify for different ages)
Time: 30 minutes
Materials: Reusable cups, outdoor space with access to natural objects, flowers, and plants
Relevant Subject: Science

1. Form groups of no more than five children and give everyone a cup. Explain that each of them will be making a "smell" tea of natural objects. Invite them to fill their cup with soil, leaves, herbs, pine needles, or berries (but *not* water), and have them stir their smell tea with a stick. Then tell them to give their tea a name. When all the teas are prepared and named, have each child pass around his or her tea and tell its name so that everyone has a chance to share their concoction before playing the Smell Tea game.

2. To play the game, have one person be "it" and put on a blindfold. One at a time each member of the group should place a cup of smell tea in the person's hands. The person who's "it" smells the tea and guesses it by name. Once he or she has had the chance to smell each tea and guess its name, the next person gets to be "it," and the game continues until everyone has had a chance to test their sense of smell.

Note: The Smell Tea game not only awakens our sense of smell, it usually elicits marvel at the variety of aromas that can be created using many of the same raw ingredients. More often than not, each tea is very distinct and easy to identify even though the participants have gathered natural objects from the same area. This activity, in addition to being fun, also builds memory skills.

FIND YOUR TREE

Grades: 3 and up
Time: 30 minutes
Materials: Outdoor space with trees, blindfolds
Relevant Subject: Science

1. To do this activity, you'll need to find some woods or a park where there are many trees. Have students pair up, and ask one person in each pair to put on a blindfold. Invite the others to carefully lead their partner on a roundabout journey to a tree they pick out for their partner to "meet." Tell the blindfolded children to feel the tree thoroughly, as high as they can reach, down at the base of the trunk, and around the perimeter. When they think they know their tree, have the partners lead them, also in a roundabout way, back to where they started.

2. Have the students remove their blindfolds and go look for their tree.

Note: Students feel an enormous sense of accomplishment when they find their tree (and most do on the first guess) and realize how much they know from their senses! Some students report that they knew which direction they were going because, despite the blindfold, they could tell where the sun was by the warmth on their skin. Others share clues they got from their feet as they traversed the terrain, and explain that they recognized where their tree was by a log they had to step over. This activity not only helps students to appreciate trees (it's difficult not to appreciate a tree one has touched and explored so carefully), but also boosts their self-confidence as they recognize their capacity to know things in ways that are different from typical academic classroom learning.

WHAT WILL YOU SAY?

Grades: 5 and up
Time: 10-20 minutes
Relevant Subjects: Social Studies, Science, and Language Arts

After a program, series of programs, course, or unit in Humane Education, ask students to close their eyes and listen as you recite the following guided visualization to them, utilizing your own words and modifying for your students as needed.

Visualization: Imagine that you are very old and at the end of your long life. You are sitting on a park bench, and the air is fresh, clean, and fragrant with flowers. You can hear the sounds of birds and crickets. You are thinking back on your life, remembering when the Earth was in grave danger, when wars, poverty, racism, ecological destruction, animal cruelty, and other forms of injustice and bigotry were commonplace. You smile, realizing that so many problems have been solved, that prejudice is a distant memory, and that people have learned to live harmoniously and sustainably on the Earth. As you are imagining these changes, a child comes up to you and joins you on the bench. This child has learned about the problems the Earth, its people, and animals once faced, and turns to you asking what you did to help make the world so much better. What will you say to this child?

2. Allow students time to fully engage in the visualization and think about their contribution.

3. Gently ask students to bring their attention back to the classroom and, when they are ready, to open their eyes.

4. Ask the students to write down their experience of the visualization.

5. Have students talk to the person next to them and share what they've written before inviting them to share with the whole class.

SIX

Suggestions for Implementing Humane Education in Schools

Getting Started

If you wish to bring humane education into your classroom or school, you may wonder exactly how to begin. Because humane education is not a subject normally taught in schools, there is no one specific way to introduce it into your curricula or classes. Matt Wildman, a Brooklyn, NY, high school teacher mentioned in Chapter One, offered his humane education course with another teacher, combining periods for history and language arts into a daily, three-hour class that met for the entire school year. Other teachers have offered semester-long humane education electives for high school students. Still others have become visiting humane educators, offering humane education classes to schools across several counties. These humane educators contact schools and work in partnership with teachers to offer lessons and classes that the teachers do not feel prepared to teach themselves. Danielle Marino, a substitute teacher and humane educator in Chicago, brings humane education lessons to her students

113

whenever she is called in to substitute. As mentioned in the FAQs, some teachers are working towards opening humane education charter schools.

As you consider the ways in which you can bring humane education to students, the following can serve as a guide:

1. Consider your options. Do you want to:
   a) Incorporate humane themes and activities into your existing curricula?
   b) Offer a humane education course or elective?
   c) Open a humane education charter school?
   d) Offer summer classes?
   e) Offer adult learning programs?
   f) Become your school's humane educator for all grades?
   g) Become your district's humane educator for several schools?
   h) Mentor an after school club on humane living?
   i) Gain further knowledge and training in humane education?

By clearly identifying your goals, you will be able to pursue a path to achieve them.

2. Meet with parents and administrators and share your vision of bringing pertinent, meaningful education about making humane life choices to your students. Invite parent involvement in setting goals for humane citizenship.

3. Define what it means to be humane by coming up with a class list of the best qualities of human beings. Explore and identify together what being humane means in the broadest, most comprehensive sense; that is, in relation to all people, all species, and the environment.

4. Make being humane a cornerstone of your class and/or school culture.

5. Place powerful, inspiring quotations about living with integrity, honesty, compassion, and respect around the classroom. Invite students to bring quotations that they find and put new ones up weekly.

6. Read the books and watch the videos listed in the Resources at the end of this book. Become more informed yourself so that you can bring vital and worthwhile humane education to your students.

7. Identify organizations and individuals that can serve as resources and guest presenters on topics related to human rights, environmental ethics, media literacy, consumer awareness, and animal protection. For controversial topics, make certain to identify individuals with different perspectives.

8. Begin using the humane education activities and suggestions in this book in your classroom.

9. Use the suggested humane education books and curricula in the resources to further expand your repertoire.

10. Evaluate your efforts. Periodically assess whether students are learning what you set out to teach them. Do they have accurate information? Are they thinking critically about it? Are they becoming more reverent, respectful, and responsible? Are you offering them positive choices?

11. Pursue continuing education by attending workshops relevant to humane education.

Humane Education Electives, After school Programs, and Summer Classes

One of the ways in which humane education can reach young people is through elective courses, after school programs, and summer classes. I personally discovered the power and promise of humane education when I taught my first humane education courses in the summers of 1987 and '88 at the University of Pennsylvania through its Discovery Program for secondary school students.

During two of the courses I taught, one on animals and the other on the environment, I witnessed students turn their curiosity and compassion into commitment and personal responsibility. One boy who was particularly upset when he learned about the testing of cosmetics on animals made homemade leaflets that night and spent his lunch hour the next day handing them out to passersby. Two others started a student activist group in Philadelphia, and to this day, both are committed and passionate citizens who try to live as humanely as possible.

After teaching these summer courses, I realized how potent such education could be. I began to offer presentations in schools, sometimes leading assembly programs, sometimes offering a series of programs for classrooms. What grew out of these individual presentations were student clubs devoted to activism and solving problems. Often these clubs hosted after school courses and classes so that students could learn more about the issues.

While teachers have busy schedules, many look forward to offering elective courses to their high school students. Such courses provide students with an opportunity to expand their intellectual horizons as well as giving the teacher the chance to explore new subject matter, become energized by relevant material, and develop innovative skills.

A humane education elective can take several forms. Ideally, the elective would meet for a minimum of three hours per week for the whole school year, but a shorter, semester-length course, can be offered instead.

A SAMPLE YEAR-LONG COURSE

SEPTEMBER-OCTOBER

Human Rights: Covering issues of prejudice (racism, sexism, homophobia, xenophobia, classism), modern-day slavery, child and sweatshop labor, political oppression, environmental racism, and poverty.

The human rights unit would offer students the opportunity to reflect upon and question their own prejudices, to learn about how societal and individual choices perpetuate or alleviate human suffering, and to practice mediation between conflicting rights and values so that they can propose solutions to entrenched problems.

NOVEMBER-DECEMBER

Cultural Issues: Covering media analysis and literacy, advertising, public relations, corporate influences in government, and any societal perspectives that impact belief systems and behaviors. This unit would enable students to be critical thinkers, to become adept at analyzing media and other messages, and to learn to resist both peer and cultural messages that would have them act in ways contrary to their deepest values.

JANUARY-FEBRUARY

Environmental Preservation: Covering pollution, habitat destruction, endangered species, resource depletion, global warming, and human overpopulation. Unlike traditional environmental studies courses, this unit would focus primarily on the dangers that our ecosystem faces and on solutions to environmental problems. This section would rely upon science, but would explore both personal and societal answers to growing environmental concerns.

MARCH-APRIL

Animal Protection: Covering uses of animals for food, clothing, entertainment, companionship, and testing. This unit would consider whether and in what ways animals ought to be spared suffering and exploitation, questioning if and when animals should be granted rights and protection, and exploring both personal and societal solutions to widespread institutionalized animal cruelty.

MAY-JUNE

Connections, Conflicts, and Meaningful Solutions: The last unit of the humane education course would draw together the connections between the previous units and explore the conflicts that arise between them. In *Biophilia*, Biologist E.O. Wilson wrote: "To choose what is best for the near future is easy. To choose what is best for the distant future is also easy. But to choose what is best for both the near and distant futures is a hard task, often internally contradictory, and requiring ethical codes yet to be formulated." So, too, to choose what is best for humans is easy. To choose what is best for animals is easy. To choose what is best for the environment is easy. But to choose what is best for humans, animals, and the environment (in both the near and distant futures) is "a hard task, often internally contradictory, and requiring ethical codes yet to be formulated." The goal of the final unit is to empower and inspire students to come up with meaningful solutions to problems and to take personal responsibility for their role in creating a humane world.

Infusing the Standard Curricula with Humane Education

As mentioned earlier, while Humane Education will achieve its greatest promise when it is taught as its own subject by trained humane educators, it is also easy and effective to incorporate humane education into the existing curricula. Teachers can use humane education techniques, lessons, and activities and still meet the objectives required by state/provincial and national standards. Be careful, however, to avoid a piecemeal approach to humane education. When you bring humane education into your curricula, draw connections between the range of issues and problems that humane education explores. Be aware, too, that your effort to model the message you want to convey will be one of the greatest lessons you will give your students. For example, in addition to simply and powerfully modeling respect and compassion for your students, you can have a classroom recycling bin, use materials that are found, recycled, or reused in your activities and lesson plans, model language that is respectful, and so on.

Below are examples of how you can make humane education relevant and use it in all the standard subject categories:

LANGUAGE ARTS

- Choose literature that explores humane themes (that is, themes like "compassion," "courage," "kindness," "integrity," "honesty," "perseverance").
- Provide writing assignments that ask students to explore how individuals can live with respect for other people, animals, and the Earth.
- Analyze and compare written materials for bias, distortions, assumptions, and stereotypes.
- Offer themes such as "justice," "compassion," "kindness," or "integrity" for writing assignments.
- Ask students to respond in writing or orally to questions offering moral dilemmas and to suggest solutions to ethical quandaries.
- Have students write about the humane education activities described in the previous section of this book.

SOCIAL STUDIES

- Study movements for social change and their effects on society, government, and culture, such as the civil rights movement, the suffragist movement, or the current movements to end human slavery and protect animals.
- Analyze themes of justice, fairness, rights, and responsibilities as they pertain to human cultures, animals, and the environment.
- Explore global issues such as the population explosion, the distribution of resources and wealth, sustainable living, and poverty.
- Examine prejudices such as racism, sexism, heterosexism, speciesism, classism, jingoism.
- Plan class/student involvement in community service and volunteer projects.
- Use guided visualizations to build empathy and appreciation for others.
- Show social change videos and analyze their messages and content (see pp. 154-155 for video suggestions).

- Analyze advertising for cultural messages (see p. 79).
- Use the Choices, True Price, Greatest Impact, Behind the Scenes, and Which to Pick? activities described in the previous section to analyze and assess the effects of personal choices on oneself and others.
- Offer the activity "What Is a Humane Life?" for students to explore positive social impacts of behavior.
- Use activities such as Cast Your Vote and Executive Commission to promote citizenship.
- Compare historical accounts of human slavery to current practices of animal slavery (see Marjorie Spiegel's, *The Dreaded Comparison*).
- Compare American slavery of the 17th and 18th centuries to modern-day slavery (see Kevin Bale's, *Disposable People*).
- Watch films that explore a range of historical atrocities (e.g., the Holocaust, genocide in Rwanda) and discuss how these atrocities could have been prevented.
- Read historical accounts of different cultures and compare the philosophies and ideologies of different societies to answer the question, "How can people live sustainably and peaceably?"

SCIENCE

- Analyze the effects of, and explore solutions to, various ecological threats (e.g., global warming, resource depletion, growing ozone holes, pollution).
- Teach principles of ecology through analyzing lifestyle choices in relation to sustainability.
- Study life through nonviolent ethology (the study of animal behavior) rather than dissection of purposefully killed animals, and use computer programs, models, and photographs to learn anatomy.
- Study the chemistry of pollution and assess clean-up needs, including measurement of water and air pollution in the neighborhood of your school.

- Read texts that explore animal behavior (through nonviolent ethological methods), such as those of Jane Goodall or Dr. Marc Bekoff.
- Create an organic school garden and composting system.
- Use web-of-life activities that demonstrate the impact on the entire web of seemingly individual stresses.
- Analyze the effects of personal product, food, and transportation choices on water, air, land, and resources through activities such as True Price and Behind the Scenes.
- Analyze the impact of trash, using the Trash Investigators activity.
- After completing a Council of All Beings, ask students to do a report on the being for whom they spoke.

MATHEMATICS

- Use the "ecological footprint" assessment to analyze human impact on the environment (see Mathis Wackernagel and William Ree's, *Our Ecological Footprint*).
- Conduct math problems based on real-world data as opposed to fabricated data, for example by calculating the population growth of humans.
- Calculate energy and/or water use in school or home and determine ways to decrease energy use.
- Study issues of population by learning key topics such as exponential versus geometric growth (see *People and the Planet*, edited by Pamela Wasserman).
- Analyze population issues in relation to dogs and cats who are not spayed/neutered.
- Do the math behind the production of things (see the activity Behind the Scenes).
- Do a cost/benefit analysis of the choices offered in the activities Choices Cards or Which to Pick?

"My Life Is My Message" Questionnaire

Mahatma Gandhi was once asked by a reporter, "What is your message." He responded, "My life is my message." Each of our lives is our message, too. While what you say as a teacher is obviously very important, who you are as a person, and how much you model compassion and respect, will be the biggest message you bring to your students. As William Ellery Channing once said, "May your life preach more loudly than your words."

The following questionnaire will give you the opportunity to reflect upon your life and put into words some concrete goals for modeling your message. This questionnaire asks you to think about the qualities that are most important to you and to consider the ways in which you live accordingly, as well as the ways in which you'd like to better embody your values. It offers you a chance to really explore your dreams for living a more humane life, to consider what holds you back, and to make some commitments to yourself. As you complete this questionnaire, try to tap into your deepest wisdom and your most ardent hopes for yourself, your family, your students, and the world we all share.

As you complete this questionnaire, you'll notice that most questions are divided into three parts: 1) What you currently do, 2) What you want to learn/do, and 3) What steps you will take. The purpose of this three-part approach is to help you a) identify the ways in which you already live according to your values, b) explore what you need to learn to live better, and c) help you make tangible plans for achieving your goals.

Initially there may not appear to be much difference between Parts Two and Three. You'll be asked in Part Two what you think you need to learn, or what you'd like to change. Then you'll be asked in Part Three to write down the steps you will take to follow through, and it may seem that you've already done this by articulating your goal. But the purpose of Part Three is to make very concrete, *very manageable* plans for yourself. Please make sure to write down only those ideas that are easy to carry through and that truly inspire you. You will notice that in Part Three there is not much room to write. This is to help you make promises to yourself that are small enough that you can keep them.

"My Life is my Message"
Questionnaire

1. The qualities (virtues) most important to me are the following:

_____ _____ _____ _____

_____ _____ _____ _____

2a. My life already reflects the following qualities fairly well:

_____ _____ _____ _____

_____ _____ _____ _____

2b. I would like to live my life so that it reflects the following qualities more deeply:

_____ _____ _____ _____

_____ _____ _____ _____

2c. In order to achieve this goal, I will take the following steps:

_____

_____

_____

3a. With my family, students, and friends, I model the following qualities:

_____

_____

3b. I would like to model the following qualities more consciously with my family, students, and friends:

_____   _____   _____   _____

_____   _____   _____   _____

3c. In order to achieve this goal, I will take the following steps:

_____

_____

4a. In relation to my health (physical, emotional, intellectual, spiritual), I take care of myself in the following ways:

_____

_____

_____

_____

_____

_____

4b. I would like to learn/do the following in order to improve my health:

_____

_____

4c. I will take the following steps to improve my health:

_____

_____

5a. In my interactions outside of home and school, my attitudes, behaviors and relationships reflect the following qualities and virtues:

_____

_____

_____

_____

5b. I would like to learn/do the following in order to improve my attitude, behaviors, and relationships:

_____

_____

_____

_____

_____

5c. I will take the following steps to improve my attitudes, behaviors, and relationships:

_____

_____

6a. In relation to activism and volunteerism, I already do the following:

_____

_____

_____

_____

6b. In relation to activism and volunteerism, I would like to help more in the following ways:

_____

_____

_____

_____

6c. I will take the following steps in order to help others through activism and volunteerism:

_____

_____

_____

7a. In relation to charitable giving and sharing my resources, I contribute in the following ways:

_____

_____

_____

_____

7b. I would like to contribute more in the following ways:

_____

_____

_____

_____

7c. I will take the following steps to contribute more:

_____

_____

8a. In relation to other people who produce and supply the products and services I use, I currently make the following choices to prevent others from suffering or being exploited:

_____

_____

_____

_____

8b. In relation to other people who produce and supply the products and services I use, I need to learn about the following in order to make choices that better reflect reverence, respect, and responsibility:

_____

_____

_____

_____

_____

8c. I will take the following steps to learn, think critically, and make more humane choices in relation to other people:

_____

_____

9a. In relation to other species (wildlife as well as domesticated animals used for food and clothing, in product testing, and in forms of entertainment, kept in shelters, etc.), I currently make the following choices to minimize animal suffering and exploitation:

_____

_____

_____

_____

9b. In relation to other species (wildlife as well as domesticated animals used for food and clothing, in product testing, and in forms of entertainment, kept in shelters, etc.), I need to learn about the following in order to make choices that better reflect reverence, respect, and responsibility:

_____

_____

_____

_____

_____

9c. I will take the following steps to learn, think critically, and make more humane choices in relation to other species:

_____

_____

10a. In relation to the environment (air, salt water, fresh water, land, soil, forests, rainforests, natural resources, etc.), I currently make the following choices to live an environmentally friendly life:

_____

_____

_____

_____

10b. In relation to the environment (air, salt water, fresh water, land, soil, forests, rainforests, natural resources, etc.), I need to learn about the following in order to make choices that better reflect reverence, respect, and responsibility:

_____

_____

_____

_____

10c. I will take the following steps to learn, think critically, and make more humane choices in relation to the environment:

_____

_____

_____

11. In order to turn the intentions I identified in this questionnaire into practical changes, I will use the following methods to support and discipline myself (this support can be internal — such as starting a meditation practice — or external — such as taking a class or creating a support group — or a combination of both):

_____

_____

_____

_____

12. Imagine a world 40 years from now in which many of the problems we face today have been solved. A child visits you and asks, "What role did you play to help make the world better?" What would you like to be able to say to this child?

_____

_____

_____

_____

_____

_____

_____

_____

_____

_____

_____

_____

_____

Facts, Stats, and Lists

In this section you'll find information, statistics, and lists that will help you educate yourself further about the issues pertinent to humane education. As I've said earlier, being a humane educator requires that you must inform yourself about a range of issues related to human rights, environmental preservation, consumer and media issues, and animal protection. Each of these subjects could be a Ph.D. program! It's impossible to know everything about all these issues and concerns, but I hope that the information that follows will get you started. Following these facts, stats, and lists you'll find resources such as recommended books, sources for relevant videos, and websites. By reading these (and other) books, watching films on topics related to humane issues, and familiarizing yourself with information from the suggested websites, you will be able to offer more accurate information to your students and expand their horizons as you expand your own.

CONSUMERISM: FACTS AND STATISTICS

These statistics are excerpted from *All Consuming Passion: Waking up from the American Dream* (3rd ed., 1998), a pamphlet produced by the New Road Map Foundation and Northwest Environment Watch. All statistics are cited and sourced in this pamphlet, which is available for $1 from the Simple Living Network (800-318-5725).

- American parents spent 40% less time with their children in 1985 than they did in 1965
- Percentage of free time spent watching TV: 40
- Amount of time the average American will spend watching TV commercials: almost 2 years of his or her life
- Amount of time the average American spends either watching TV or behind the wheel of a car: the equivalent of one day out of every week
- Number of high schools in the U.S. in 1996: 24,000
- Number of shopping centers in the U.S. in 1996: 42,130

- Average time per week spent shopping in the U.S. in 1985: 6 hours
- Average time per week spent playing with children in the U.S. in 1985: 40 minutes
- Number of new toys issued each year by American toymakers: 3,000 to 6,000
- Spending on toy advertising:
    1983: $357 million
    1993: $878 million
- Americans spend twice as much on children's athletic shoes than they do on children's books.
- By the time they are 3 years old, most children are making specific requests for brand-name products.
- Percentage rise in per capita income in the U.S. since 1970: 62
- Percentage decrease in quality of life in the U.S. since 1970, as measured by the Index of Social Health: 51
- Percentage of Americans making over $100,000 a year who agree with the statement, "I cannot afford to buy everything I really need:" 27
- Median size of a new house built in the U.S.:
    1949: 1,100 square feet
    1970: 1,385 square feet
    1996: 1,950 square feet
- Household size in the U.S.:
    1970: 3.14 persons per household
    1995: 2.65 persons per household
- Percentage of disposable personal income in the U.S. allotted to savings:
    1980: 8.2
    1995: 4.5
    1997: 2.1
- Americans' share of the world population: 5%
- It would require four Earths for everybody on the planet to have the lifestyle of North Americans.

- Since 1940 Americans have used up as large a share of the earth's mineral resources as all previous humans put together.
- The U.S. has lost:
  50% of its wetlands
  85% of its old-growth forests
  99% of its tallgrass prairie
  up to 520 species of native plants and animals, with another 6,000 now being at risk.
- Per capita American consumption of soft drinks in 1989: 47 gallons
- Per capita American consumption of tap water in 1989: 37 gallons
- Total energy consumed in producing a 12-ounce can of diet soda: 2,200 calories
- Total food energy in a 12-ounce can of diet soda: 1 calorie
- The amount of energy used by one American is equivalent to that used by:
  3 Germans
  6 Mexicans
  14 Chinese
  38 Indians

DO-IT-YOURSELF CLEANING RECIPES

General Household Cleaner: Mix 3 tablespoons baking soda into 1 quart warm water, or mix white vinegar and salt for surface cleaning, or pour vinegar and baking soda onto damp sponge.

Glass Cleaner: Mix equal parts white vinegar and water in a spray bottle and use newspaper rather than cloth to rub windows.

Linoleum Floor Cleaner: Mop with 1 cup white vinegar mixed with 2 gallons of water.

Furniture Polish: Mix 3 parts olive oil and 1 part vinegar, or 1 part lemon juice with 2 parts olive oil, and use a soft cloth.

Drain Opener: Pour ½ cup baking soda, then ½ cup vinegar down drain — also use this combination as a general toilet bowl cleaner, but do *not* combine with store-bought toilet cleaners.

Oven Cleaner: While oven is warm, pour salt on dirty areas then scrape dirt off after oven has cooled. For harder-to-clean areas, spray with vinegar-water solution and add baking soda on top. Rub gently with steel wool and rinse.

Air Freshener: Leave open a box of baking soda in room, or add cloves and cinnamon to boiling water and simmer.

SWEATSHOP-FREE AND FAIR TRADE CLOTHES AND PRODUCTS

Coop America's website (<www.coopamerica.org>) maintains an up-to-date list of companies which do and those which do not employ sweatshop labor. They also publish their national *Green Pages* (<www.greenpages.org>) which lists companies that adhere to fair trade and environmental standards. The *Green Pages* includes lists of companies that sell organic and environmentally friendly foods, products, and clothing. Please visit these websites for information on specific companies and products. Coop America has also created a checklist that consumers can use when they visit retail stores.

Coop America's Checklist for Sweatshop-Free Products

Ask the companies with which you do business the following questions:
- Does your company know how the workers who made this product were treated?
- Do you have a list of all the factories around the world that make your products?
- Does it include the wages and working conditions in each factory?
- Can I see the list?
- Does your company guarantee that the workers who made this product were paid a living wage, or enough to support their families?

- Are you providing development programs in the communities where your workers live?
- Does your company have a code of conduct that protects human rights and forbids child labor and unsafe conditions in all the factories that make its products?
- How do you enforce these rules?
- Are your factories monitored by independent, third-party sources?
- Are you working with others in your industry to come up with truthful, meaningful labels so consumers can know exploited labor wasn't involved in making your products?

GENETICALLY ENGINEERED FOODS

The non-profit organization Greenpeace maintains an up-to-date website (<www.truefoodnow.org>) to inform consumers about which food companies do and which do not use genetically engineered ingredients. To find out whether the foods you buy contain genetically modified organisms (GMOs), you can visit this website. Since labeling GE foods is not required by law, it is up to consumers to find out whether or not their foods contain GMOs. You can use the suggested questions below as a guide when contacting companies.

To find out company policies and ingredients, you can call companies using their toll-free phone numbers, usually printed on the food packaging.

Ask the company these three questions (from the <truefoodnow.org> website):

1. Does your company support the consumer's right to know if foods are made with genetically engineered ingredients or ingredients derived from genetically engineered crops?
2. Does your company currently inform consumers on your labels whether you use genetically engineered ingredients or ingredients derived from genetically engineered crops in your products?

3. Does your company intend to eliminate genetically engineered ingredients and ingredients derived from genetically engineered crops from its products?

DIETARY CHOICES: STATISTICS ON HUMAN HEALTH, THE ENVIRONMENT, WORLD HUNGER, AND ANIMALS

These statistics are compiled from John Robbins' *The Food Revolution* (2002). While I have not included citations, each statistic is carefully sourced and documented in Robbins' book.

Health and Diet
- Percentage of adult daily value for saturated fat in one Double Whopper with cheese: 130
- Percentage of eight-year-old child's daily value for saturated fat in one Double Whopper with cheese: more than 200
- Risk of death from heart disease for vegetarians compared to nonvegetarians: half
- Blood cholesterol levels of complete vegetarians (who consume no meat, fish, dairy, or eggs) compared to those of nonvegetarians: 35% lower
- Percentage of patients with high blood pressure who are able to completely discontinue use of medications after adopting a low-sodium, low-fat, high-fiber vegetarian diet: 58
- Amount spent annually by Kellogg's to promote Frosted Flakes: $40 million
- Amount spent annually by the dairy industry on the "milk mustache" ads: $190 million
- Amount spent annually by McDonald's to advertise its products: $800 million
- Amount spent annually by the National Cancer Institute to promote the consumption of fruits and vegetables: $1 million
- Countries with the highest consumption of dairy products: Finland, Sweden, U.S., England
- Countries with the highest rates of osteoporosis: Finland, Sweden, U.S., England

- Daily calcium intake for African-Americans: more than 1,000 mg
- Daily calcium intake for black South Africans: 196 mg
- Hip fracture rate for African-Americans compared to that of black South Africans: 9 times greater
- Calcium intake in rural China: ½ that of people in the U.S.
- Bone fracture rate in rural China: ⅕ that of people in the U.S.
- Foods that when eaten produce calcium loss through urinary excretion: animal protein, salt, and coffee
- Amount of calcium lost in the urine of a woman after she has eaten a hamburger: 28 mg
- Amount of calcium lost in the urine of a woman after she has had a cup of coffee: 2 mg
- Number of antibiotics allowed in U.S. cow's milk: 80
- Average American's estimate when asked what percentage of adults worldwide does not drink milk: 1
- Actual percentage of adults worldwide who do not drink milk: 65
- Leading cause of food-borne illness in the U.S.: Campylobacter
- Number of people in the U.S. who become ill with Campylobacter poisoning every day: more than 5,000
- Number of annual Campylobacter-related fatalities in the U.S.: more than 750
- Primary source of Campylobacter bacteria: contaminated chicken flesh
- Percentage of American chickens sufficiently contaminated with Campylobacter to cause illness: 70
- Percentage of American turkeys sufficiently contaminated with Campylobacter to cause illness: 90
- Number of hens in three commercial flocks screened for Campylobacter by University of Wisconsin researchers: 2,300
- Number of hens not infected with Campylobacter: 8
- Number of Americans sickened from eating Salmonella-tainted eggs every year: more than 650,000
- Number of Americans killed from eating Salmonella-tainted eggs every year: 600

- Percentage increase in Salmonella poisoning from raw or undercooked eggs between 1976 and 1986: 600
- Amount of antibiotics administered to people in the U.S. annually to treat diseases: 3 million pounds
- Amount of antibiotics administered to livestock in the U.S. annually for purposes other than treating disease: 24.6 million pounds
- Amount of minerals in organic food compared to conventional food:

Calcium	63 % greater
Chromium	78 % greater
Iodine	73 % greater
Iron	59 % greater
Magnesium	138 % greater
Potassium	125 % greater
Selenium	390 % greater
Zinc	60 % greater

Environmental Concerns

- Amount of water required to produce 1 pound of California foods, according to Soil and Water specialists, University of California Agricultural Extension, working with livestock farm advisors:

1 pound of lettuce	23 gallons
1 pound of tomatoes	23 gallons
1 pound of potatoes	24 gallons
1 pound of wheat	25 gallons
1 pound of carrots	33 gallons
1 pound of apples	49 gallons
1 pound of chicken	815 gallons
1 pound of pork	1,630 gallons
1 pound of beef	5,214 gallons

- Number of calories of fossil fuel expended to produce 1 calorie of protein from soybeans: 2
- Number of calories of fossil fuel expended to produce 1 calorie of protein from corn or wheat: 3

- Number of calories of fossil fuel expended to produce 1 calorie of protein from beef: 54
- Amount of waste (stored in open cesspools) produced by North Carolina's 7 million factory-raised hogs compared to the amount produced by the state's 6.5 million people: 4 to 1
- Relative concentration of pathogens in hog waste compared to human sewage: 10 to 100 times greater

World Hunger

- Number of people whose food energy needs can be met by the food produced on 2.5 acres of land:

if the land is producing cabbage	23 people
if the land is producing potatoes	22 people
if the land is producing rice	19 people
if the land is producing corn	17 people
if the land is producing wheat	15 people
if the land is producing chicken	2 people
if the land is producing eggs	1 person
if the land is producing beef	1 person

- Amount of grain needed to adequately feed every person on the entire planet who dies of hunger and hunger-caused disease annually: 12 million tons
- Percentage by which Americans would have to reduce their beef consumption to save 12 million tons of grain: 10

Animal Suffering

- Mass of breast tissue of eight-week-old chicken today compared with 25 years ago: 7 times greater
- Percentage of broiler chickens who are so obese by the age of six weeks that they can no longer walk: 90
- Number of U.S. pigs raised for meat: 90 million
- Number of U.S. pigs raised in total confinement factories where they never see the light of day until being trucked to slaughter: 65 million

- Percentage of U.S. pigs who have pneumonia at time of slaughter: 70
- Average number of days newborn calves stay with their mothers: 1
- Space provided to milk-fed veal calves for the duration of their 4 month lives: enough to take one step forward and one back, but not enough to turn around
- Cage floor space provided to hens used to produce eggs in modern battery-cage facilities: barely more than the size of this book

Animal Testing: A Partial List of Companies that Do NOT Test their Products on Animals (2003)

ABBA Products, Inc.

Abracadabra, Inc.

Aubrey Organics

Aura Cacia, Inc.

Auromere Ayurvedic Imports

Autumn Harp, Inc.

Avalon Organic Botanicals

Aveda

Avon Products, Inc.

Ayurveda Holistic Center

Axtec Secret

Banana Boat Products

Bath & Body Works

Beauty without Cruelty

Biogime Int'l, Inc.

The Body Shop

Brookside Soap Co.

Clear Vue Products, Inc.

Clearly Natural Products, Inc.

Clinique

Conair Corporation

Compassionate Consumer

Crabtree & Evelyn, Ltd.

Deodorant Stones of America

Desert Naturels

Dr. Broner's "All One" Products

Dr. Hauschka Cosmetics

Earth Science, Inc.

Ecco Bella

EcoSafe

Ecover Products

Eden Botanicals

Estée Lauder Co.

Bon Ami Company

Frank T. Ross & Sons, Ltd.

Giogio

Green Ban

HERC Consumer Products
Home Service Products Co.
Jason Natural Cosmetics
Jean Naté
John Paul Mitchell Systems
Jojoba Resources, Inc.
Kiss My Face
KMS Research, Inc.
KSA Jojoba
Levlad, Inc.
Life Tree Products
Lotus Light Enterprises
Louice Bianco Skin Care, Inc.
Marcal Paper Mills, Inc.
Mary Kay Cosmetics
Naturade
Natural Bodycare
Naturally Yours, Alex
Nature's Gate
Nature's Plus
Nexxus Products Company
Nirvanan, Inc.
Norelco
Oasis Brand Products
Orange-Mate, Inc.
Orjene Cosmetic Co., Inc.
Oxyfresh Worldwide, Inc.
Pamela Marsen, Inc.
Paul Penders
Peelu Products, Inc.
PetGuard
Pets 'N People, Inc.

Rachel Perry, Inc.
Rainforest Essentials
Redken Laboratories, Inc.
Reviva Labs, Inc.
Revlon, Inc.
Santa Fe Fragrance, Inc.
Sappo Hill Soapworks
SerVaas Labs, Inc.
Seventh Generation
Shaklee U.S., Inc.
Shikai Products
Sierra Dawn
Simplers Botanical Co.
Sinclair & Valentine
Sleepy Hollow
Sonoma Soap Company
St. Ives Labs, Inc.
Sumeru Garden Herbals
Sunshine Natural Products
Terra Nova
Tisserand Aromatherapy
Tom's of Maine
Trader Joe's Company
Ultima II
Unpetroleum
Vegelatum
Vermont Soapworks
Weleda, Inc.
Wella Corporation
WiseWays Herbals
Wysong Corp.
Yves Rocher, Inc.

In addition, look on individual products for the Corporate Standard of Compassion for Animals logo.

For more information, contact:
Coalition for Consumer Information on Cosmetics
P.O. Box 75307
Washington, DC 20013
1-888-546-CCIC

CCIC identifies companies that have pledged they will neither conduct or commission animal tests on finished products nor use any ingredient formulation that is tested on animals.

Resources

Recommended Books

Humane Education

Bekoff, Marc. *Strolling with our Kin*. AAVS, 2000.

Bigelow, Bill and Bob Peterson. *Rethinking Globalization: Teaching for Justice in an Unjust World*. Rethinking Schools Press, 2002.

Brookfield, Stephen D. *Developing Critical Thinkers*. Jossey-Bass, 1987.

Chaffee, John. *The Thinkers Way*. Little Brown, 1998.

Christensen, Linda and Stan Karp. *Rethinking School Reform: Views from the Classroom*. Rethinking Schools Press, 2003.

Clarke, Tony and Sarah Dopp. *Challenging McWorld*. Canadian Centre for Policy Alternatives, 2001.

Cornell, Joseph. *Sharing Nature with Children*. Dawn Publications, 1979.

Garbarino, James. *Raising Children in a Socially Toxic Environment*. Jossey-Bass, 1995.

Gatto, John Taylor. *Dumbing Us Down*. New Society Publishers, 1992.

Hammond, Merryl and Rob Collins. *One World, One Earth: Educating Children for Social Responsibility*. New Society Publishers, 1993.

Herman, Marina, Joseph Passineau, Ann Schimpf, and Paul Treuer. *Teaching Kids to Love the Earth.* Pfeifer-Hamilton, 1991.

Jukes, Nick and Mihnea Chiuia, *From Guinea Pig to Computer Mouse.* InterNICHE, 2003.

Lickona, Thomas. *Educating for Character: How our Schools can Teach Respect and Responsibility.* Bantam, 1991.

Luvmour, Sambhava and Josette. *Everyone Wins! Cooperative Games and Activities.* New Society Publishers, 1990.

Miller, Alice. *For Your Own Good: Hidden Cruelty in Childhood and the Roots of Violence.* Trans. Hildegarde and Hunter Hannum. Farrar, Strauss, Giroux, 1983.

Miller, Ron. *Caring for New Life.* Foundation for Educational Renewal, 2000.

National Science Teachers Association. *The Life Cycle of Everyday Stuff.* National Science Teachers Association Press, 2001.

National Wildlife Federation and Population Communications International. *The Cost of Cool: Youth, Consumption and the Environment — A Resource Guide for High School Educators.* National Wildlife Federation and Population Communications International, 2002.

Palmer, Parker. *The Courage to Teach.* Jossey-Bass, 1998.

Pike, Graham and David Selby. *In the Global Classroom* (Books 1 and 2). Pippin Publishing, 1999.

Rivera, Michelle. *Canines in the Classroom.* Lantern Books, 2004.

Seed, John, Joanna Macy, Pat Fleming, and Arne Naess. *Thinking Like a Mountain: Toward a Council of All Beings.* New Society Publishers, 1988.

Selby, David. *EarthKind: A Teachers Handbook on Humane Education.* Trentham Books, 1995.

Sheehan, Kathryn and Mary Waidner. *EarthChild: Games, Stories, Activities, Experiments & Ideas About Living Lightly on Planet Earth.* Council Oaks Books, 1994.

Swope, Kathy and Barbara Miner. *Failing Our Kids: Why the Testing Craze Won't Fix our Schools.* Rethinking Schools Press, 2000.

Van Matre, Steve. *Earth Education: A New Beginning.* Institute for Earth Education, 1990.

Wasserman, Pamela, ed. *People and the Planet: Lessons for a Sustainable Future.* Zero Population Growth, 1996.

Weil, Zoe. *Above All, Be Kind: Raising a Humane Child in Challenging Times.* New Society Publishers, 2003.

Weil, Zoe. *Animals in Society: Facts and Perspectives on our Treatment of Animals.* Animalearn, 1990.

Weil, Zoe. *So, You Love Animals: An Action-Packed, Fun-Filled Book to Help Kids Help Animals.* Animalearn, 1994.

Media and Consumer Issues

Bagdikian, Ben. *The Media Monopoly.* Beacon Press, 1995.

Best, Joel. *Damned Lies and Statistics.* University of California Press, 2001.

Consumers Union Education Services. *Captive Kids: Commercial Pressures on Kids at School.* Consumers Union Education Services, 1995.

De Graaf, John, David Wann, and Thomas H. Naylor. *Affluenza: The All-Consuming Epidemic.* Berrett-Koehler, 2001.

General Accounting Office. *Public Education: Commercial Activities in Schools.* U.S. General Accounting Office, 2000.

Jacobson, Michael F. and Laurie Ann Mazur. *Marketing Madness.* Westview Press, 1995.

Kilbourne, Jean. *Can't Buy My Love.* Simon and Schuster, 1999.

Klein, Naomi. *No Logo.* Picador, 1999.

Korten, David. *When Corporations Rule the World.* Kumarian Press, 1995.

Lasn, Kalle. *Culture Jam.* William Morrow, 1999.

Mander, Jerry. *Four Arguments for the Elimination of Television.* William Morrow, 1978.

McChesney, Robert W. *Rich Media, Poor Democracy.* University of Illinois Press, 1999.

McKibben, Bill. *The Age of Missing Information.* Plume, 1993.

Molnar, Alex. *Giving Kids the Business: The Commercialization of America's Schools.* Westview Press, 1996.

Quart, Alissa. *Branded: The Buying and Selling of Teenagers.* Perseus, 2003.

Quinn, Bill. *How WalMart is Destroying America.* Ten Speed Press, 1998.

Quinn, Daniel. *Ishmael.* Bantam/Turner, 1992.

Postman, Neil. *Amusing Ourselves to Death.* Penguin, 1985.

Stauber, John and Sheldon Rampton. *Toxic Sludge Is Good for You.* Common Courage Press, 1995.

Steyer, James P. *The Other Parent: The Inside Story of the Media's Effect on Children.* Atria Books, 2002.

Summers, Sue Lockwood. *Media Alert! 200 Activities to Create Media-Savvy Kids.* Hi Willow Research and Publishing, 1997.

Welton, Neva and Linda Wolf. *Global Uprising: Confronting the Tyrannies of the 21st Century.* New Society Publishers, 2001.

Winn, Marie. *The Plug-In Drug.* Penguin, 1985.

Human Rights

Bales, Kevin. *Disposable People.* University of California Press, 2000.

Ehrenreich, Barbara and Arlie Russell Hochschild. *Global Woman: Nannies, Maids, and Sex Workers in the New Economy.* Metropolitan, 2002.

Faludi, Susan. *Backlash: The Undeclared War Against American Women.* Anchor, 1991.

Fuller, Robert W. *Somebodies and Nobodies: Overcoming the Abuse of Rankism.* New Society Publishers, 2003.

Jensen, Derrick. *The Culture of Make Believe.* Context, 2002.

Johnson, Allan G. *Privilege, Power and Difference.* McGraw Hill, 1997.

Kielburger, Craig. *Free the Children*. HarperPerennial, 1998.

Kressel Neil J. *Mass Hate: The Global Rise of Genocide and Terror*. Westview Press, 2002.

Schlosser, Eric. *Fast Food Nation*. Houghton Mifflin, 2001.

Shiva, Vandana. *Stolen Harvest: The Hijacking of the Global Food Supply*. South End Press, 2000.

Szwarc, Josef. *Faces of Racism*. Amnesty International, 2001.

Social Change

Abdullah, Sharif. *Creating a World that Works for All*. BK Publishers, 1999.

AtKisson, Alan. *Believing Cassandra: An Optimist Looks at a Pessimist's World*. Chelsea Green, 1999.

Callander, Meryn G. and John W. Travis. *A Change of Heart*. Arcus Publishing, 1993.

Elgin, Duane. *Voluntary Simplicity*. William Morrow, 1993.

Hammond, Allen. *Which World?: Scenarios for the 21st Century*. Island Press, 1998.

Hartmann, Thom. *The Last Hours of Ancient Sunlight*. Mythical Books, 1998.

Jones, Ellis, Ross Haenfler and Brett Johnson, with Brian Klocke. *The Better World Handbook: From Good Intentions to Everyday Actions*. New Society Publishers, 2001.

Loeb, Paul Rogat. *Soul of a Citizen*. St. Martin's Press, 1999.

Robbins, Ocean and Sol Solomon. *Choices for Your Future*. Book Publishing, 1994.

Shi, David. *The Simple Life*. Oxford University Press, 1985.

Seo, Danny. *Be the Difference: A Beginner's Guide to Changing the World*. New Society Publishers, 2001.

Environmental Issues

Carson, Rachel. *Silent Spring.* Houghton Mifflin, 1962.

Dauncey, Guy. *Stormy Weather: 101 Solutions to Global Warming.* New Society Publishers, 2001.

Erhlich, Paul and Anne. *Betrayal of Science and Reason.* Island Press, 1996.

Goldbeck, Nikki and David. *Choose to Reuse.* Ceres Press, 1995.

Greer, Jed and Kenny Bruno. *Greenwash: The Reality Behind Corporate Environmentalism.* Third World Press, 1996.

Hawken, Paul. *The Ecology of Commerce.* HarperBusiness, 1993.

Meadows, Donella and Denis and Jorgen Randers. *Beyond the Limits.* Chelsea Green, 1992.

Orr, David. *Earth in Mind.* Island Press, 1994.

Reeske, Mike and Shirley Watt Ireton. *The Life Cycle of Everyday Stuff.* NSTA Press, 2001.

Ryan, John C. and Alan Thein Durning. *Stuff: The Secret Lives of Everyday Things.* Northwest Environment Watch, 1997.

Shiva, Vandana. *Water Wars.* South End Press, 2002.

Tobias, Michael. *World War III.* Continuum, 1998.

Wackernagel, Mathis and William Rees. *Our Ecological Footprint.* New Society Publishers, 1996.

Worldwatch Institute. *State of the World* books. Worldwatch Institute.

Animal Issues

Cavialleri, Roberto and Peter Singer. *The Great Ape Project.* St. Martins Press, 1993.

Donovan, Josephine and Carol Adams, eds. *Beyond Animal Rights.* Continuum, 1996.

Eisnetz, Gail. *Slaughterhouse.* Prometheus, 1997.

Goodall, Jane and Marc Bekoff. *The Ten Trusts: What We Must Do to Care for the Animals We Love.* Harper San Francisco, 2002.

Mason, Jim. *An Unnatural Order*. Continuum, 1997.

Masson, Jeffrey Moussaieff with Susan McCarthy. *When Elephants Weep*. Delacorte, 1995.

Newkirk, Ingrid. *Free the Animals*. Noble Press, 1992.

Patterson, Charles. *Eternal Treblinka: Our Treatment of Animals and the Holocaust*. Lantern Books, 2002.

Scully, Matthew. *Dominion*. St. Martin's Press, 2002.

Singer, Peter. *Animal Liberation*. Avon, 1975.

Spiegel, Marjorie. *The Dreaded Comparison*. Mirror Books, 1996.

Health and Diet

Barnard, Neal. *The Power of Your Plate*. Book Publishing, 1990.

Lappé, Frances Moore. *Diet for a Small Planet*, 20th anniversary ed. Ballantine, 1991.

Lappé, Marc and Britt Bailey. *Against the Grain: Biotechnology and the Corporate Takeover of Your Food*. Common Courage Press, 1998.

Lyman, Howard with Glen Merzer. *Mad Cowboy*. Scribner, 1998.

Marcus, Erik. *Vegan: The New Ethics of Eating*. McBooks, 1998.

McDougal, John. *The McDougal Program for a Healthy Heart*. Dutton, 1996.

Ornish, Dean. *Dr. Dean Ornish's Program for Reversing Heart Disease*. Ivy Books, 1996.

Robbins, John. *The Food Revolution*. Conari Press, 2002.

Cookbooks

Barnard, Tanya and Sarah Kramer. *How it All Vegan*. Arsenal Pulp Press, 2000.

McCarthy, Meredith. *Sweet and Natural*. St. Martins Press, 1999.

Pickarski, Brother Ron. *Friendly Foods*. Ten Speed Press, 1991.

Robertson, Robin. *Vegan Planet*. Harvard Common Press, 2003.

Sass, Lorna. *Complete Vegetarian Kitchen*. Hearst Books, 1992.

Stepaniak, Joanne and Kathy Hecker. *Ecological Cooking*. Book Publishing, 1991.

Stepaniak, Joanne. *The Uncheese Cookbook*. Book Publishing, 1994.

Tucker, Eric and John Westerdahl. *The Millennium Cookbook*. Ten Speed Press, 1998.

Recommended Periodicals

The Atlantic Monthly	*Orion*
Green Teacher	*The Progressive*
E Magazine	*Satya*
Earth Island Journal	*Utne*
Encounter: Education for Meaning and Social Justice	*Yes! A Journal of Positive Futures*
Extra!	*Veg*News*
Hope Magazine	*WorldWatch*
Mother Jones	*Z Magazine*
Multinational Monitor	
New Internationalist	

Recommended Videos

For selections of videos on human rights, social justice, and environmental issues:

> Bullfrog Films <ww.bullfrogfilms.com>

> Video Project <www.videoproject.net>

For selections of videos on media issues:

> Media Education Foundation <www.mediaed.org>

For selections of videos on animal issues:

Farm Sanctuary <www.farmsanctuary.org>

People for the Ethical Treatment of Animals
<www.peta-online.org>

Tribe of Heart <www.tribeofheart.org>

Organizations and Websites

The list of websites below includes non-profit organizations that attempt to alleviate suffering, raise awareness, and prevent destruction. This list does not include industry sites or groups funded largely by industry. When you look at the list below, my bias becomes clear: I want you to have information about protecting our planet, its people, and its animals. This choice of websites is also meant to balance the perspectives that are promoted by well-funded industries and by the expensive curricula that these industries are providing free of charge to schools. The inclusion of these websites does not imply that these are the only sources of information on these topics; rather, they are meant to offer alternative views to industry opinions. For corporate perspectives, you can usually go to the website listed on a specific product. There are also industry-represented groups whose goal is to promote the use of certain resources or products (e.g., coal, nuclear energy, paper, biomedical research); you can find these sites by simply doing a search on the subject, for example "coal" or "nuclear energy."

Humane Education

American Forum for Global Education <www.globaled.org>

American Humane Association <www.americanhumane.org>

AnimaLearn <www.animalearn.org>

Association for Professional Humane Educators <www.aphe.humanelink.org>

Bridges of Respect <www.bridgesofrespect.org>

Center for Non-Violent Communication <www.cnvc.org>

Changing Consumption Patterns <www.sustainabilityed.org>

Circle of Compassion <www.circleofcompassion.net>

The Empathy Project <www.empathyproject.org>

The E.T.H.I.C. <www.the-ethic.org>

Healing Species <www.healingspecies.org>

Humane Education Advocates Reaching Teachers
<www.nyheart.org>

International Institute for Global Education <www.oise.utoronot.ca>

International Institute for Humane Education <www.IIHEd.org>

International Network for Humane Education <www.interniche.org>

The Latham Foundation for the Promotion of Humane Education
<www.Latham.org>

National Association for Humane and Environmental Education
<www.nahee.org>

National Coalition of Education Activists <www.nceaonline.org>

New World Vision <www.newworldvision.org>

Rethinking Schools <www.rethinkingschools.com>

Roots and Shoots <www.janegoodall.org/rs>

Seeds for Change Humane Education
<www.seedsforchangehumaneeducation.org>

TeachKind <www.teachkind.org>

Yes! Tour <www.yesworld.org>

Sustainable Living
A Better Future <www.abetterfurture.org>

Center for New American Dream <www.newdream.org>

Earth Future <www.earthfuture.org>

Population Coalition <www.popco.org>

Redefining Progress <www.rprogress.org>

Simple Living Network <www.simpleliving.net>

Simply Enough <www.simplyenough.com>

SustainUS <www.sustainus.org>

Media

Adbusters Media Foundation <www.adbusters.org>

Center for Commercial-Free Public Education <www.igc.org>

Center for Media Education <www.cme.org>

Commercial Alert <www.commercialalert.org>

Fairness and Accuracy in Reporting <www.fair.org>

National Institute on Media and the Family
<www.mediaandthefamily.org>

PR Watch <www.prwatch.org>

Stop Commercial Exploitation of Children
<www.commercialexploitation.com>

TV Turnoff Network <www.tvturnoff.org>

Human Rights and Social Justice

Amnesty International <www.amnesty.org>

Anti-Slavery International <www.antislavery.org>

Coop America <www.coopamerica.org>

Fair Trade <www.fairtrade.org>

Free the Children <www.freethechildren.org>

Global Exchange <www.globalexchange.org>

Human Rights Watch <www.hrw.org>

The Hunger Project <www.thp.org>

Independent Media Center <www.indymedia.org>

Infact <www.infact.org>

International Forum on Globalization <www.ifg.org>

Oxfam <www.oxfam.org>

Sustainable Harvest International <www.sustainableharvest.org>

United Students against Sweatshops <www.usasnet.org>

Environment

Circle of Life Foundation <www.circleoflifefoundation.org>

Earth Island Institute <www.earthisland.org>

Ecological Footprint of Nations
 <www.ecouncil.ac.cr/rio/focus/report/english/footprint/>

Friends of the Earth <www.foe.org>

GRACE <www.gracelinks.org>

Greenpeace <www.greenpeace.org>

Leadership for Environment and Development <www.lead.org>

Native Forest Council <www.forestcouncil.org>

Rainforest Action Network <www.ran.org>

Student Environmental Action Coalition <www.seac.org>

Worldwatch Institute <www.worldwatch.org>

Animal Protection

Animal Protection Institute <www.api4animals.org>

Compassion Over Killing <www.cok.net>

Doris Day Animal League <www.ddal.org>

Endangered Species Coalition <www.stopextinction.org>

Farm Sanctuary <www.farmsanctuary.org>

Farm Animal Reform Movement (FARM) <www.farmusa.org>

Fund for Animals <www.fund.org>

Humane Society of the United States <www.hsus.org>

In Defense of Animals <www.idausa.org>

International Fund for Animal Welfare <www.ifaw.org>

People for the Ethical Treatment of Animals <www.peta-online.org>

Tribe of Heart <www.tribeofheart.org>

United Poultry Concerns <www.upc-online.org>

Food and Diet

Earthsave <www.earthsave.org>

Safe Tables Our Priority (STOP) <www.stop-usa.org>

Food First <www.foodfirst.org>

Center for Food Safety <www.centerforfoodsafety.org>

Organic Consumers Association <www.purefood.org>

Pesticide Action Network <www.panna.org>

North American Vegetarian Society <www.navs-online.org>

Greenpeace's True Food shopping list <www.truefoodnow.org>

Vegan Outreach <www.veganoutreach.org>

VegSource Interactive <www.VegSource.com>

Scientists and Doctors for Reform

Center for Science in the Public Interest <www.cspinet.org>

Ethologists for the Ethical Treatment of Animals
<www.ethologicalethics.org>

Physicians Committee for Responsible Medicine <www.pcrm.org>

Physicians for Social Responsibility <www.psr.org>

Psychologists for the Ethical Treatment of Animals
<www.pyseta.org>

Canadian Assoc. of Physicians for the Environment
<www.children.cape.ca>

Union of Concerned Scientists <www.ucsusa.org>

Political Reform

Accurate Democracy <www.accuratedemocracy.com>

America Speaks <www.americaspeaks.org>

Campaign Finance Reform <www.publicagenda.org>

Common Dreams <www.commondreams.org>

Public Citizen <www.citizen.org>

Index

Acknowledgments

Comprehensive humane education is a relatively new movement that is being co-created by numerous individuals and organizations. I cannot possibly name all the people who have influenced and taught me, and who have contributed to the growth of humane education or the ideas in this book. Apologies in advance to all those whom I am leaving out of these acknowledgments. Please know that I am exceedingly grateful for all of you humane educators pioneering this critical movement.

The activities and ideas in this book come only in part from me. Many were developed and imagined by creative teachers and humane educators, while others were inspired by or modified from other people's lessons and programs. First and foremost, I'd like to thank Rae Sikora, the co-founder of the International Institute for Humane Education, with whom I worked for eight years and from whom I learned more than I can say. Rae is a spectacular humane educator, and her innovative activities can be found throughout this book.

In 1988, I had the privilege of meeting my first humane educator, Melissa Feldman. We worked together at the Women's Humane Society in Philadelphia for only nine months, but we've been collaborating ever since. I not only respect Melissa for her integrity and open-minded attitudes toward people and new ideas but am very grateful for her friendship over these past sixteen years.

Our staff at the International Institute for Humane Education (IIHE) are some of the most wonderful people I know, and I consider them among my closest friends. It is an honor and a joy to work with them. I am indebted to Khalif Williams, our executive director, and grateful every day that he has chosen to give IIHE not only his dedicated service but also his considerable talent, intelligence, and wit. My gratitude is boundless. Mary Pat Champeau, the coordinator of both our M.Ed. and Humane Education Certificate Program, is a godsend. Her equanimity, humor, and wisdom not only make our programs thrive, but also are a standard toward which I will forever strive. Dani Dennenberg is the first graduate of IIHE's M.Ed. program, and upon her graduation we promptly hired her as faculty because she is not only an excellent humane educator, she is also the quintessential maven, going above and beyond the call of duty to help our students and make their experience in our programs the best it can be. Kathy Kandziolka, the coordinator and trainer for our *Sowing Seeds* humane education workshops, is one of the most genuine, life-filled, and radiant people I've ever met. She's the kind of teacher who is unforgettable. Daniella Tessier, who works in our office part-time and otherwise runs an animal sanctuary, will one day be declared a saint, if not by a religious institution, then at least by me. Her commitment to do good in this world, despite any obstacles, is inspiring. To the members of IIHE's board — Edwin Barkdoll, Andie Locke, and Matt Wildman — thank you for your commitment to IIHE and for the help you generously provide. And to Caryn Ginsberg, IIHE's treasurer, what can I say? IIHE is so very fortunate to have you on board that I cannot begin to describe my thanks.

Somehow IIHE manages to attract to our graduate and certificate programs the most amazing people. Perhaps the greatest perk of this work is the fabulous students who come into my life. Of course, it's not simply those of us at IIHE who are blessed to know and learn from these students — they are the future of humane education. Without a doubt, they will make this movement grow and thrive.

Many of the activities in this book originated from the very earliest pioneers of comprehensive humane education, including Jon Schottland, Sara Martin, and Elizabeth Stevens. Although I've lost contact with these excellent teachers, I still rely upon their creative ideas.

To Freeman Wicklund, humane educator extraordinaire, thank you for your willingness always to stretch yourself and grow. Your brilliance, commitment, and talent, coupled with your openness and self-reflection, are among the most important qualities in creating and offering quality humane education.

IIHE would never have been able to achieve what we have achieved in such a short time were it not for Steve Komie. His commitment to humane education and his enormous generosity are a blessing for which I am eternally grateful. Humane education is spreading rapidly largely because of the fuel that Steve continues to provide. In addition, Marjo and Jim Kannry and Brad Goldberg deserve special mention. I'm incredibly appreciative of their help, commitment, and support.

To the readers of the first draft of this book — Edwin Barkdoll, Marc Bekoff, Mary Pat Champeau, Dani Dennenberg, Melissa Feldman, Bruce Friedrich, Caryn Ginsberg, Andie Locke, Mary Ann Naples, Matt Wildman, Khalif Williams, and Yale Wishnick — thank you so much! Your careful review and suggestions have made it so much better, and I'm very grateful for the time and effort you put into your comments and critiques.

Speaking of Mary Ann Naples, this book began with her. I don't know if all agents so enthusiastically encourage and support their clients, read several versions of their manuscripts, and help them every step of the way. If not, I'm immensely lucky. Thank you Mary Ann — I'm honored to be represented by you.

New Society Publishers is one of the few publishing companies whose goal is to improve the world. I've been reading and learning from New Society books for years, and we use several of them as texts for students in our programs. What a privilege to now be among their authors. Many thanks to Chris and Judith Plant, Justine Johnson, Heather Wardle, Michael Mundhenk, Sue Custance, and all those NSP staff members who have helped bring my books to the public.

To researchers who are bringing the plight of the Earth, animals, and all people to light, thank you. Without you we would not have the information we need to teach the next generation. To activists working to alleviate suffering and destruction on this planet, thank you. Without you we would not have role models to emulate and encouragement to live up to the challenges of creating peace.

I do my work with the love and assistance of my husband Edwin Barkdoll, and with the acute awareness that the world I am trying to help create is the one our son Forest will inherit. I would do this work anyway, but having Edwin's support and the humbling knowledge that my efforts directly affect my own son empowers, encourages, and inspires me far more than if I were doing this work without them in my life.

About the International Institute for Humane Education

The International Institute for Humane Education (IIHE) is dedicated to creating a world where kindness, respect, and compassion are the guiding principles in our relationships with all people, animals, and the Earth. IIHE works to achieve this goal by training individuals to be humane educators and advancing comprehensive humane education worldwide.

In 1997, IIHE created the first Humane Education Certificate Program (HECP) in the United States, and, in 2000, began offering a distance-learning Master of Education degree in Humane Education through an affiliation with Cambridge College, also a first in the U.S. IIHE leads weekend *Sowing Seeds* humane education workshops in the United States and Canada and each year trains hundreds of people to be humane educators who, in turn, reach thousands of students.

Headquartered in Surry, Maine, IIHE is situated on 28 oceanfront acres overlooking the mountains of Acadia National Park. The grounds include an organic garden, a woods trail, and a pebble beach where seals, eagles, loons, and osprey are frequently seen.

To learn more, please visit <www.IIHEd.org> or send an email to info@IIHEd.org.

About the Author

ZOE WEIL is co-founder and
president of the International
Institute for Humane Education
(IIHE) and the author of
*Above All, Be Kind: Raising a
Humane Child in Challenging
Times.* A humane educator since
1985, Zoe now trains others to
be humane educators through
IIHE's graduate and certificate
programs in humane education. Zoe received master's degrees
from Harvard Divinity School and the University of Pennsylvania.
She and her husband, Edwin Barkdoll, live in coastal Maine with
their son and several rescued animals. You can visit IIHE's website
at <www.IIHEd.org> or contact Zoe at zoe@IIHEd.org.

A book that transforms children's natural
love and compassion for animals into positive action

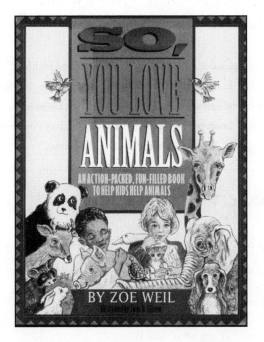

So, You Love Animals
Raising a Humane Child in Challenging Times
ZOE WEIL

So, You Love Animals teaches 9-12 year olds what is happening to other species, enabling them to turn their care for animals into effective and positive choices that improve their lives. Covering companion animals, farmed animals, those used in entertainment, sport, experimentation and wildlife, it engages kids with facts, games, skits, experiments and exciting activities, empowering them to make a difference.

192 PAGES 7.5 X 9" 50 B&W ILLUSTRATIONS
NATURE & NATURAL HISTORY / ENVIRONMENTAL STUDIES /
EDUCATION & TEACHING
ISBN 1-88169-901-3 US$14.95 / CAN$19.95

If you have enjoyed *The Power and Promise of Humane Education*,
you might also enjoy other

BOOKS TO BUILD A NEW SOCIETY

Our books provide positive solutions for people who want to
make a difference. We specialize in:

Sustainable Living • Ecological Design and Planning

Natural Building & Appropriate Technology • New Forestry

Environment and Justice • Conscientious Commerce

Progressive Leadership • Resistance and Community • Nonviolence

Educational and Parenting Resources

New Society Publishers

ENVIRONMENTAL BENEFITS STATEMENT

New Society Publishers has chosen to produce this book on recycled paper made with 100%
post consumer waste, processed chlorine free, and old growth free.

For every 5,000 books printed, New Society saves the following resources:[1]

39	Trees
3,533	Pounds of Solid Waste
3,887	Gallons of Water
5,070	Kilowatt Hours of Electricity
6,422	Pounds of Greenhouse Gases
28	Pounds of HAPs, VOCs, and AOX Combined
10	Cubic Yards of Landfill Space

[1]Environmental benefits are calculated based on research done by the Environmental Defense Fund and
other members of the Paper Task Force who study the environmental impacts of the paper industry.
For more information on this environmental benefits statement, or to inquire about environmentally
friendly papers, please contact New Leaf Paper – info@newleafpaper.com Tel: 888 • 989 • 5323.

For a full list of NSP's titles, please call **1-800-567-6772** *or check out our web site at:*

www.newsociety.com

NEW SOCIETY PUBLISHERS